A Spiritual Formation Guide for People with Intellectual Disabilities From A Christian Perspective

By: Dr. Wesley Don Cohoon

This guide is a resource that allows ministers and laypeople to come alongside those with intellectual disabilities for a mutual ministry of giving and receiving.

Acknowledgements

This spiritual formation guide came about from my work as a chaplain with adults who have intellectual disabilities. Undertaking and reflecting on this guide has enabled my appreciation for my brothers and sisters with cognitive impairments to continue to grow. They are my friends, co-laborers in ministry, and teachers, who continually show me what it means to love God with all of one's heart, mind, and strength.

I would like to offer special thanks to my wonderful wife, Amber, who continues to support and encourage me. When we first met, I was neither in ministry nor a Christian, and I did not have any academic degrees. She is a life-transforming presence and pillar in my life.

The faculty of Logsdon Seminary at Hardin-Simmons University has also been a great source of support and motivation. Dr. Steve Lyon journeyed with me as both a friend and a mentor. My predecessor, Dr. Dennis Schurter, set the foundation for my current ministry with his 30 years of faithful service. This project would not be possible without my friends and partners in ministry Feby Mathew and Brett Koltuniak. Lastly, I am grateful to all of the pastoral care professionals who contributed to this project: William Gaventa, Dr. Dennis Schurter, Dr. Paul Kraus, Bill Starcher, Tom Dowdy, Karen Hulsey, Dr. Keith Robinson, and Bobby Hendricks.

Contents

Introduction

This guide is for people in the ministry with others who have intellectual disabilities and those who are interested in such a life-changing endeavor. It is not created to be a meticulous or rigid guide that handles every situation and tells people exactly what to do. Instead, the guide is a resource that allows ministers and laypeople to come alongside those with intellectual disabilities for a mutual ministry of giving and receiving. My hope is the readers will employ their own personality, gifting, and calling to fulfill the ministry where the Lord has them.

This guide divides into five parts. The first part establishes a theological rationale that undergirds and informs a ministry with people with intellectual disabilities. The theological foundation is not intended to be exhaustive, and there might be areas where the reader wishes would have more depth. However, the design offers the necessary framework needed to provide a God-honoring ministry that partners, not oppresses, people with intellectual disabilities.

After the theological foundation, the guide moves into the practice of ministry. The practical part builds from the theology by offering tools and approaches. The practice of ministry section expressly provides concepts for those in this type of work while still allowing for contextualization of personality, situation, systems, and culture. The central thesis of this guide is that people grow spiritually primarily through relationships. While this guide is intended for ministry with people with intellectual disabilities, I feel very convinced that the concepts, theology, and practices apply to everyone.

The third section of the guide gives a ministry evaluation tool. Many times we perform pastoral tasks with little guidance or understanding of how to measure success or performance. How do people know if they are doing what God has called them to do? Ministry is people-centric work and cannot always have specific outcomes, but that does not mean that we need to abandon assessment tools altogether. The questions in the evaluation section are designed to measure and cause deeper reflection for the practice of ministry.

The last two sections of the guide offers practical examples of how this guide works in the real world. I took the research and example from my Doctor of Ministry Project to illustrate how this guide could look and be evaluated when it is applied.

You are invited to read, engage, and perform the concepts in this guide with a critical eye. My clinical training as a chaplain employed the action-reflection model where a person completes an action, reflects, learns new information, and then goes out to perform the task again. For me, the action-reflection model is very helpful for life and ministry. My hope is that you employ a similar concept with this guide.

There are things that you may disagree with in this guide, and that is ok. Perhaps we have different experiences or beliefs. However, I invite you to engage, reflect, and then integrate what is valid for you and your ministry setting. If you are uncomfortable with some things in here, I hope you continue onward and reflect what about the alternate view or practice is so troubling. No matter what you believe, I trust that your love, acceptance, flexibility, and consistency with people who have intellectual disabilities is the most important factor regarding their spiritual health.

Have fun and may God be with you!

Theological Foundation

Truthfulness and honesty are part of theological integrity. While people from the same denomination or church may profess identical doctrinal stances, each person usually emphasizes certain Scriptures or truths more than others. I am no different in my approach. I have blind spots, favorite passages, and individual elements of practical theology that work best for my ministry setting. The primary theological rationale chosen for this guide includes the "living human document," Scripture, image of God, moral behavior, and community.

The Theological Starting Point

Love is the starting place. No matter what a person does or does not do, love is at the center. The Apostle Paul correctly highlights this truth in his letter to the church in Corinth:

> *If I speak in tongues of men or of angels, but do not have love, I am only a resounding gong or a clanging cymbal. If I have the gift of prophecy and can fathom all mysteries and all knowledge, and if I have a faith that can move mountains, but do not have love, I am nothing. If I give all I possess to the poor and give over my body to hardship that I may boast, but do not have love, I gain nothing (1 Corinthians 13:1-3).*

The above passage applies very much to ministry and specifically ministry with people who have intellectual disabilities. This Scripture reminds us that love is more important than any spiritual gifting, knowledge, faith, and selfless act. If you are going to make an error in ministry, it is best to error on the side of love.

Love is the binoculars that a person looks through while Scripture and a person's story are the lens. You must have a foundation of love and then view the situation through the Bible and the person's history. This approach takes a person's culture and bias into perspective. Understanding a person's history is what Anton Boisen (the founder of clinical pastoral education movement) referred to as the "living human document." Boisen advocated that the first theological task starts with the individual and the social complexities instead of written materials.[1] Even the authors of Scripture approached their writings with a distinct worldview in a particular time in history.

The minister's primary job is to read the "living human document." This does not occur through finding an objective form of truth or reality, but instead, discovers what the client or parishioner understands life to be. This approach deconstructs any hierarchy. The minister is not the expert of the truth. He or she is a fellow learner alongside the person. The minister is not the one who brings God. Instead, they uncover God's current presence and work.

Therefore, the first theological task is not preaching but listening to people's stories.[2] Even if one's primary ministry is teaching, people

---

[1] Anton Boisen, *The Exploration of the Inner World: A Study of Mental Disorder and Religious Experience* (Philadelphia: University of Pennsylvania Press, 1971), 185.

[2] Hans Reinders, *Disability, Providence, and Ethics: Bridging Gaps, Transforming Lives* (Waco: Baylor University Press, 2014), 10.

cannot be taught until their lives are heard. Attending to people's stories accomplishes a few things. First, listening is good practice and honors the image of God in the other person. Second, it allows the teacher to connect with his audience. Third, listening transforms an inherent hierarchical relationship into a mutual responsive relationship where both people give and receive.

While understanding the other person is paramount, biography and autobiography are instrumental in constructing a disability theology.[3] People with severe intellectual disabilities experience oppression and a violation of rights through able-bodied people defining and categorizing them. Instead of seeing disability as a tragedy or a blessing, it is important to let the person with an intellectual disability speak for himself or herself. It can be challenging when dealing with someone who is non-verbal and has a profound intellectual disability. However, with patience and active listening, a minister allows people to share their life and experiences.

There are many ways to let people who are non-verbal with severe intellectual disabilities speak for themselves. Have a normal conversation with them. Say hello and ask how they are doing. As the person is sitting there, use personal touch through placing a hand on their shoulder. Patiently listen and make eye contact. Engage in a mini-conversation through

---

[3] Tabita Kartika Christiani, "Doing Theology: Towards the Construction of Methods of Living with Disability," *Asia Journal of Theology* 28, no. 1 (April 2014): 42.

complimenting what they are wearing or what they are doing that day. It is not that hard, but it does require care and imagination.

In addition to the "living human document," Scripture is the second theological foundation. The two are not mutually exclusive. They build and complement one another. Intertwining the truth of an individual's experience with the truth of Scripture allows both to have a transformational impact. The Bible is not a far removed ancient document, but a living relevant text.

One way that the Bible is overused by some religious groups is that it is considered primarily a tool for salvation, like the famous Romans Road passages. The problem with this approach for people who have intellectual disabilities is that it does not help them grow spiritually. Individuals with intellectual disabilities get to know Jesus not through agreeing to statements of fact, but instead, trusting the person who is ministering to them.

Spiritual formation for adults with intellectual disabilities is not a New Testament Epistle where everything follows a tidy outline: all beginnings are similar, the body of teaching is a comprehensive list of propositional truths, and everything concludes with final instructions. An epistle approach to discipleship does not take nuances into account. Instead, spiritual growth is more similar to an Old Testament historical narrative or a Gospel account. People lose their place along the journey and progress is not always linear.

Some people struggle with how to use Scripture with people who have intellectual disabilities. At a basic level, the Bible communicates God's guidance, love, and presence. One of my favorite examples of using the Bible with people who have cognitive impairments occurs during our Sunday morning services. Many of our residents get a new Bible each week, or they bring their Bible. After they accumulate several Bibles, we reuse and re-gift them. Every Sunday, the people I minister to want a new Bible. I affirm that it is God's special book that tells us how much he loves us and how to live.

One Sunday, I noticed a resident holding a Bible upside down as her finger went over the words. I sat by her and asked if she knew what it said. She said, "No." I put my finger on the upside down words and read, "God love you." I emphatically told her that it was saying God personally loves her. She became very excited, smiled, and said, "Me?!" She was able to learn a profound biblical truth without in-depth Bible study. The minister needs to let go of preconceived ideas and listen to those whom he or she serves for these opportunities to impact the other person.

This guide starts with the premise of God's option for the poor, a view rooted in Scripture, which means God has preferential treatment for the marginalized. Understanding the impact that marginalization, mental health, and intellectual disabilities have on people is necessary. Engaging in the undercurrents of social, psychological, and political issues helps identify oppressive realities in Scripture and current systems.[4]

Therefore, the guide advocates reading Scripture with empathy. How did the marginalized people feel who are in passages? Where is the Bible or the characters of the Scripture oppressive? How are we, as ministers and persons in authority, oppressive to those whom we serve? These questions are not intended to vilify anyone but create self-awareness and connection with Scripture and those we serve. After we can see biblical narratives from various vantage points, we may begin reflecting about how to teach and where to learn from people who are marginalized.

Another consideration with Scripture and the "living human document" is understanding that there are many different ways to teach the Bible. Sometimes a lesson may involve reading or talking. But for people with cognitive impairments, actions are sometimes the best lessons. It does not have to be a planned or rehearsed action, but instead, look for opportunities to love, serve, and learn.

Every Sunday, people enthusiastically show up to the chapel where I serve. Sometimes in the morning excitement, they may have missed a button, put the tie over their collar, or missed another wardrobe detail. Privately reminding them to fix their clothes, or simply fixing it yourself, is a simple way that communicates God's love and care.

---

[4] Scot Danforth, "Liberation Theology of Disability and the Option for the Poor," *Disability Studies Quarterly* 25, no. 3 (Summer 2005): 3-6.

God cares for the oppressed. The two charts below illustrate two examples. The first one shows that God is in the center of injustice, with the poor, the vulnerable, and everyone else. While God loves everyone, Scripture teaches that He has a special place for those who are considered weaker and less fortunate.

God Cares for the Oppressed

Poor

Looking at his disciples, he said: "Blessed are the poor, for yours is the kingdom of God." Luke 6:20

Vulnerable

"Do not take advantage of a widow or an orphan." Exodus 22:22

God

Injustice

"They trample on the heads of the poor as upon the dust of the ground and deny justice to the oppressed... Now then, I will crush you as a cart crushes when loaded with grain." Amos 2:7, 13

Everyone Else

"For God so loved the world that he gave his one and only son..."

John 3:16

The second image shows the prevalent view and Jesus' view of God's kingdom. The religious leaders thought they were at the center of God's kingdom, but Jesus reoriented them. Jesus placed the children, poor, blind, and disabled at the center, while the religious leaders were at the edge. The below chart serves as a sober reminder that God's view of success is different from the world's. People with intellectual disabilities are the utmost importance to God.

Popular Structure of God's Kingdom[5]

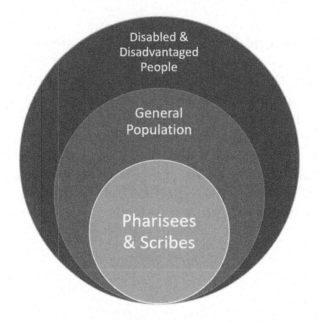

[5] Dennis D. Schurter, *A Mutual Ministry: Theological Reflections and Resources on Ministry with People with Mental Retardation and Other Disabilities* (Denton: Dennis D. Schurter, 1994), 23.

Jesus' Structure of God's Kingdom

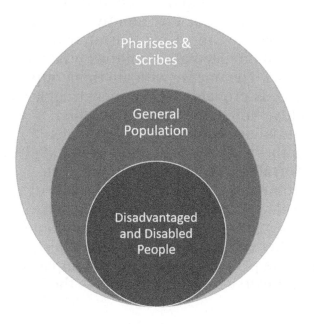

Another central part of this guide's theological rationale is that all people are made in the image of God or *imago Dei*. I frequently encounter able-minded people expressing tension with how or if those with intellectual disabilities reflect the *imago Dei*. The unease with anything outside of normalcy is probably rooted in a struggle with mortality, vulnerability, and limitation. Unfortunately, an able-bodied person's discomfort with his or her feelings of inadequacy and mortality can force individuals with developmental disabilities into the role of the scapegoat.[6] Scapegoating happens when someone places insecurity, fear, and contempt on another person, people, group, object, or event. The person with a cognitive impairment does not worry if he or she reflects the image of God.

Human's Unique Relationship

---

[6] Thomas E. Reynolds, *Vulnerable Communion: A Theology of Disability and Hospitality* (Grand Rapids: Brazos Press, 2008), 110.

Imago Dei is not an ability, but being in a relationship.

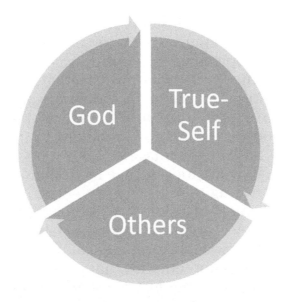

The *imago Dei* is not an ability found in humans like intellect, emotion, or will. Instead, the image of God reflects humans' unique relationship with God.[7] The problem with linking particular qualities with *imago Dei* is that, if a person does not or cannot represent those capacities, then he or she is deemed to lack the image of God. This approach dehumanizes an entire section of the population such as the elderly, individuals with intellectual disabilities, children, and people with debilitating conditions. Instead of approaching the *imago Dei* as something to earn and work towards,

---

[7] Jason D. Whitt, "In the Image of God: Receiving Children with Special Needs," *Review & Expositor* 113, no. 2 (May 2016): 210-211.

recognizing the intrinsic value of all humans honors God and humans.

God made everyone for communion with Him in unique and extraordinary manners. There are no tiers or a relational hierarchy that a person achieves. People have different ways of being in a relationship. In this view, intellectual disability is not the result of sin or the fallen *imago Dei.*[8] A person with a profound intellectual disability who is non-verbal and non-ambulatory still perfectly reflects the image of God. People with intellectual disabilities engage in a relationship through offering their presence to others.

People project ideas of perfection onto God because of insecurity and uncomfortableness with weakness. The central biblical truth is not that God is omnipotent, but that God is all-loving.[9] Therefore, the *imago Dei* fully expresses itself in relationships of love, not power. Love renders a person's cognitive function or ability irrelevant. God requires His children to imitate love and care for others.

The image of God does not wait to shine through a person with a disability when his or her body and mind is glorified in the next life. Redemption occurs when a person with an intellectual disability is free to be himself or herself.[10] Scripture does not indicate what people will be like in heaven. Any list of attributes

---

[8] Molly C. Haslam, *A Constructive Theology of Intellectual Disability: Human Being as Mutuality and Response* (New York: Fordham University Press, 2012), 94-95.

[9] Thomas H. Graves, "The Role of Despair and Anger in Christian Spirituality," *Review & Expositor* 113, no. 2 (May 2016): 186.

[10] Amos Yong, *The Bible, Disability, and the Church: A New Vision of the People of God* (Grand Rapids: William B. Eerdmans Publishing Company, 2011), 103.

changes based on the period and culture.[11] A twenty-first-century view of the redeemed body in the afterlife is different from centuries before. A capable few do not own the *imago Dei*. All of humanity reflects God's image through being in a relationship.

Too many times people with intellectual disabilities are told that they need to conform to another set of behaviors or standards. It seems like this conforming has more to do with the able-minded person's comfort than the care or personhood of the person with the cognitive impairment. Since people with intellectual disabilities frequently experience oppression, redemption for them occurs when differences and individuality are celebrated. A worship service with people who have intellectual disabilities should not be constrained by do's and don'ts, but instead, a welcoming and accepting environment that communicates the love and grace of God.

Ethical Living

The connection between right belief and right action is a major part of this theological justification. The action-reflection model found in clinical pastoral education is also applicable to right doctrine and practice. In the action-reflection approach, a person acts, reflects on the practice through Scripture and community, and emerges with new insight to engage again. While both right doctrine and right action are

---

[11] David Andurus, "Theology and Its Impact on People with Disability: An Ecclesiology Inclusive of People with a Disability," *Missio Apostolica* 18, no. 2 (2010): 146.

connected, principled action is more important than gaining esoteric knowledge. Ethical living is a central theological foundation for this guide.

While many well-known Bible verses deal with the tension of right doctrine and ethical living, this guide only chooses two. The texts selected fit for practical reasons and matched the ministry setting. First, both verses (Micah 6:8 and James 1:27) are straightforward and simple enough that the people with intellectual disabilities and their staff can use and understand them. These verses also illustrate a genuine and foundational faith that pleases God and applies in a pluralistic setting. Micah 6:8 has three primary applications for the individuals: act justly, love mercy, and walk humbly with God. James 1:27 shows the foundation of true religion: look after the oppressed and hurting while abstaining from evil.

In the passage Micah passage, the preceding verses provide a fuller picture:

> With what shall I come before the LORD and bow down before the exalted God? Shall I come before him with burnt offerings, with calves a year old? Will the LORD be pleased with thousands of rams, with ten thousand rivers of olive oil? Shall I offer my firstborn for my transgression, the fruit of my body for the sin of my soul? He has shown you, O mortal, what is good. And what does the LORD require of you? To act justly and to love mercy and to walk humbly with your God (Micah 6:6-8).

This section deals with God's expectation of humankind. Micah argues that ethical behavior is the LORD's preference, not sacrifice.[12] Verse eight answers the previous two verses through stating that God requires mercy, justice, and walking humbly. Micah reframes his audience's prominence on ritualistic activity into the importance of ethical living.

The phrase, "O mortal," connects people outside of Israel and includes all humans.[13] Micah outlines a brief baseline of behavior that anyone can follow. Sacrifice becomes irrelevant if ethical living is missing. Ethical living is not limited to the people of God, but instead, all humans are to live in a righteous manner with others.

The passage starts with animals and ends with potential child sacrifice to illustrate the absurdity of ritual behavior without justice. A higher quantity and quality of sacrifice is not always better. To prove his point, Micah contends that a firstborn child will surely please the Lord if God desires magnitude and excellence of sacrifice.[14] Micah starts with something good that is familiar to his audience, offering sacrifices according to Israel's worship. However, to show the limitations of action without mercy and justice, he takes his point to

---

[12] Bruce K. Waltke, *A Commentary on Micah* (Grand Rapids: William B. Eerdmans Publishing Company, 2007), 364.

[13] Ibid., 390.

[14] James D. Nogalski, *The Book of the Twelve: Micah-Malachi.* Smyth & Helwys Bible Commentary (Macon: Smyth & Helwys Publishing Inc., 2011), 573.

the extreme and suggests something deplorable, child sacrifice.

Perhaps a modern parallel to Micah's argument is intellectualism and a focus on right doctrine. If right teaching pleases God, maybe God will be more satisfied with the additional information. The cycle ends with a person thinking that knowledge and academic achievement impress God. The focus on ethical living brings equality to those who have an intellectual disability. This belief places everyone on an equal level. The question shifts from right doctrine to what a person does based on the knowledge he or she is given.

The previous verse in this New Testament passage of James adds to the power of the disciple's message:

> *Those who consider themselves religious and yet do not keep a tight rein on their tongues deceive themselves, and their religion is worthless. Religion that God our Father accepts as pure and faultless is this: to look after orphans and widows in their distress and to keep oneself from being polluted by the world (James 1:26-27).*

The book of James is the only wisdom literature in the New Testament. James 1:26-27 functions as a theoretical summary of the letter's ethical views.[15] Reminiscent of Old Testament Law and Prophets, several elements such as the poor and oppressed are mentioned in James. Verse 27's mandate to care for widows

---

[15] Scot McKnight, *The Letter of James.* The New International Commentary of the New Testament (Grand Rapids: William B. Eerdmans Publishing Company, 2011), 162.

and orphans connects back to the Torah in Exodus 22:22.[16] James is similar to Micah 6:8 because ethics serves as the primary component of the religious life.

For James, faith is visible through compassion, holiness, controlled speech, heartfelt responses, and abstinence from worldly sins.[17] People of different functional levels can respond in faith in a manner that is consistent with James' mandate of true religion. Individuals from a contemporary culture can forget that the focus on intellect is relatively new. The construct of intellectual disabilities did not exist before the modern era.[18] In an agrarian society, the challenge was not a person's IQ, but his or her ability to contribute to the family and community. Those unable to provide were lumped in with the poor.

In addition to James citing the Torah to prove the need to care for the oppressed and marginalized, he builds an argument. The culmination of James' ethical stance is interpreted as pure religion. He includes meekness, applying the Word of God, living the law of liberty, and bridling one's tongue.[19] Christianity devoid of care for the vulnerable is not an authentic faith. A next step in the process of caring moves from a ministry of pity to co-laboring together for Christ.

The incarnation of God dictates that Christians engage in a similar ministry as Jesus did. James

---

[16] Ibid., 168.

[17] Ibid., 164.

[18] Michael L. Wehmeyer, *The Story of Intellectual Disability: An Evolution of Meaning, Understanding, and Public Perception* (Baltimore: Paul H. Brooks Publishing Co, 2013), 48.

[19] LeeAnn Snow-Flesher, "Mercy Triumphs Over Judgment: James as Social Gospel," *Review & Expositor* 111, no. 2 (May 2014): 183-184.

writes to "keep oneself from being polluted by the world." This, however, does not mean a disengagement or separation from society.[20] The world functions through oppressing the vulnerable and seeking personal interests. The world infantilizes and disrespects individuals with cognitive impairments. Being in an equal relationship with them contrasts the world's pollution. Additionally, a Christian keeps clean by rejecting ideologies that oppress and pursue selfishness. If people are open to the type of relationship James talks about, the connection transforms all parties involved. This includes persons with disabilities and the able-bodied.

Community

In addition to the "living human document," Scripture, *imago Dei,* and ethics, equality through community provides a significant element of the theological rationale for this guide. I chose 1 Corinthians 12:21-26, with particular attention to verses 22 and 23, as the foundational Scriptural passage for the community part of the rationale. The thought that some parts of the body are "weaker" or "less honorable" connects with particular approaches to disability ministry. One emphasizes *ministry to* people who are disabled while the other method seeks to do *ministry with* people who have disabilities. Individuals with cognitive impairments serve as a different area of the

---

[20] James L. Boyce, "A Mirror of Identity: Implanted Word and Pure Religion in James 1:17-27," *Word & World* 35, no. 3 (Summer 2015): 219.

body than someone with full intellectual functioning.

This essential Scripture sets up a model of equality using the human body as an analogy:

> *The eye cannot say to the hand, "I don't need you!" And the head cannot say to the feet, "I don't need you!" On the contrary, those parts of the body that seem to be weaker are indispensable, and the parts that we think are less honorable we treat with special honor. And the parts that are unpresentable are treated with special modesty, while our presentable parts need no special treatment. But God has combined the members of the body and has given greater honor to the parts that lacked it, so that there should be no division in the body, but that its parts should have equal concern for each other. If one part suffers, every part suffers with it; if one part is honored, every part rejoiced with it (1 Corinthians 12:21-26).*

The Apostle Paul seems to address his personal bias and leanings inadvertently in verse 23. His use of "we" instead of "you" implies Paul's struggle that some parts of the body are less valuable.[21] In hierarchical social relations, it is natural to assess the importance and value of different members based on giftedness and contribution. Especially in a North American mindset of autonomy, disability brings out fears and cultural assumptions. This starting place assumes that members with intellectual disabilities have little to offer the congregation.

---

[21] Jeff McNair, "Disability Studies Applied to Disability Ministry," *Review & Expositor* 113, no. 2 (May 2016): 164.

Ending with that idea is the same as proclaiming that the whole body is an eye and has no need for the other parts.

Establishing a hierarchy with the supposed superior over the seemingly inferior harms the entire body. The Apostle Paul probably refers to the internal organs when writing about the apparent weaker. Ironically, unknown to Paul and the people of his period, the internal body parts are more necessary than the visible, external ones.[22] For instance, if a person looks at an arm as opposed to a stomach, the arm would appear primary. However, the stomach is an absolute necessity.

The body requires all of its members. Life is not full of unlimited options. The weaker members of society are often victims of others who proclaim self-determination. Net income or job titles do not measure the fruitful life. Accepting limits and the need for others is necessary.[23] The people of God gain identity, worth, and meaning through mutual growth, love, and understanding. Individuals with intellectual disabilities are no different from anyone else.

[22] Gordon D. Fee, *The First Epistle of the Corinthians: Rev. ed.*, The New International Commentary of the New Testament (Grand Rapids: William B. Eerdmans Publishing Company, 2014), 675.

[23] Parker Palmer, *Let Your Life Speak: Listening for the Voice of Vocation* (San Francisco: Jossey-Bass Publishers, 1999), 42.

The Practice of Ministry

Relationships and presence are key determinants of spiritual growth. I hypothesize that people develop spiritually through relationships – with each other and God – rather than through intellect. The areas of theory that undergird this guide's practice of ministry are relational discipleship, disability ministry, a personal theory of pastoral care, and the role music and worship play with intellectual disabilities. I firmly believe that people with intellectual disabilities are similar to those who have fully functional minds. The primary difference between the two is that those with cognitive impairments may need additional supports to engage fully in the spiritual life.

Relational Discipleship

The fundamental concept behind the guide is that spiritual formation occurs through relational discipleship. God is the original author and leader of a relational paradigm. Since the Garden of Eden, faith in God and God's promises were based on relationships.

Jesus continued to lead in the relational paradigm to spirituality. Jesus' call to discipleship, practice of ministry, and teaching about the Kingdom of God all reflect a relational style. The concept of allowing the relational and practical to influence the doctrinal did not start and stop with Him. Historical Anabaptists believed that doctrinal truths needed confirmation through practical discipleship.[24]

---

[24] Stuart Murray, *The Naked Anabaptist: The Bare Essentials of a Radical Faith* (Scottdale: Herald Press, 2010), 58.

The practice of personally knowing Jesus over knowing information about Jesus is an example of the relational paradigm to spirituality.

Throughout his ministry, Jesus' call is simply, "follow me."[25] He does not send his disciples to the synagogue for additional learning, but instead, invites them into a personal relationship with him. The Greek *akoloutheo* used by the authors in these instances of "follow me," suggests a lasting relationship, an invitation to discipleship and personal attachment.[26] A spiritual formation strategy missing the deep interpersonal connection of Jesus and community produces nothing more than people who know interesting biblical trivia.

Jesus grew his disciples through immersion in real-life circumstances and then guided them in reflection of their experiences.[27] While Jesus retrained and corrected his disciples, relationships remained his the primary focus. An alternate approach to the action-reflection model used by Jesus is a perpetual teaching model where the student continues to gain knowledge.

---

[25] Jesus uses the word, "follow me," in these subsequent instances: telling people to let the dead bury their own dead, Matthew 8:22 and Luke 9:59; calling of Levi, Matthew 9:9, Mark 2:14, and Luke 5:27; taking up the cross, Matthew 10:38; denying self in Luke 16:24, Mark 8:34, and Luke 9:23; talking to the rich young man, Matthew 19:21, Mark 10:21, and Luke 18:22; calling of Philip and Nathanael to ministry, John 1:43; being the light of the world, John 8:12; describing that Jesus' sheep follow him, John 10:27; preaching that people who serve Jesus must follow him, John 12:26; restoring Peter, John 21:19, 22.

[26] Leon Morris, *The Gospel According to Matthew* (Grand Rapids: William B. Eerdmans, 1992), 85.

[27] Brad A. Binau, "Pastoral Theology for the Missional Church: From Pastoral Care to the Care of Souls," *Trinity Seminary Review* 34, no. 1 (Spring 2014): 22. For a more exhaustive treatment, see also Reggie McNeal, *The Present Future: Six Tough Questions for the Church* (San Francisco: Jossey-Bass, 2003), 85.

The problem with such an approach is that people stay in the novice state. They do not move into the practitioner phase because there is always something else to learn before engaging in ministry. In contrast, the action-reflection model takes the focus off what a person knows and emphasizes putting that knowledge into practice.

Knowledge can impair one's relationship with God. In Matthew 18:1-5, Mark 10:13-16, and Luke 18:15-17, Jesus teaches that the Kingdom of God belongs to those who are like little children. The promise of Christ is that the greatest in the kingdom keep a childlike attitude towards Jesus and his kingdom.[28] While the church knows this teaching, the temptation remains to downplay the role of children and those who cannot contribute in traditional ways. If the kingdom belongs to children, then their approach of awe and simplicity needs to be mirrored and sought after. While adults who have intellectual disabilities are not children, they offer and teach the church regarding faith, love, and simplicity.

The role of presence is often not valued or understood. To balance this misperception, clinical training for ministers tries to teach clergy the benefits that presence offers. According to the Association of Clinical Pastoral Education Manual, a student is supposed to demonstrate a non-anxious and non-judgmental presence.[29] When a person experiences crisis,

---

[28] H. N. Ridderbos, Matthew, Bible Student's Commentary, trans. Ray Togtman (Grand Rapids: Zondervan 1987), 353.

[29] Manual Writing Committee, "Standards 311-312 Outcomes of CPE Level I/Level II Programs. Pastoral Competence: 312.6," ACPE Standards & Manual (Decatur: Association of Clinical Pastoral Education,

additional anxiety can be contagious. Instead, a minister serves as a calming presence. The emphasis over what a person does over who a person is misaligns the soul.[30] In relational discipleship, being takes priority over doing. What people do should flow from who they are. We mix this up in modern society, and usually, what a person does defines worth. One example is the modern question that comes up when we meet a new person, "So, what do you do?" Society values and assesses a person's significance based on what they do. Relational discipleship flows from personhood and presence.

Inc., 2016), accessed July 18, 2016, www.acpe.edu/ACPE/Resources/Resources_.aspx.
  [30] David Benner, *Presence and Encounter: The Sacramental Possibilities of Everyday Life* (Grand Rapids: Brazos Press, 2014), 58.

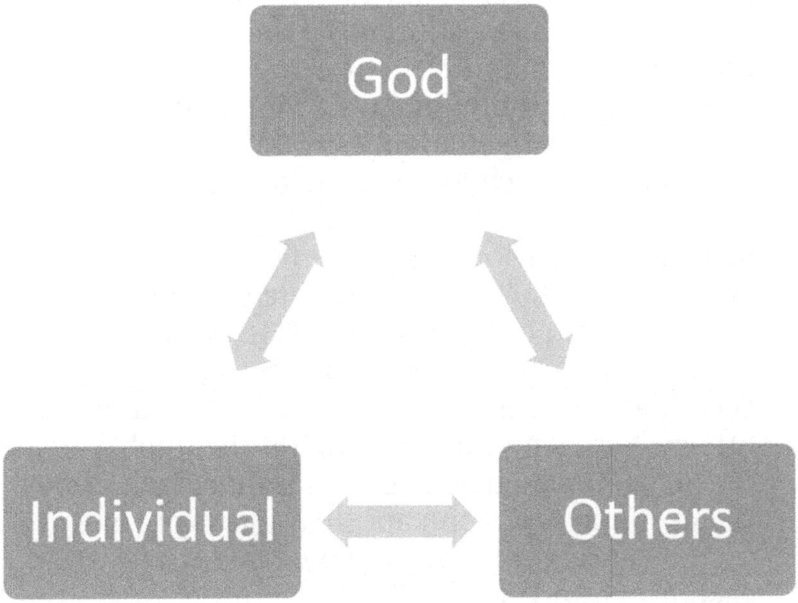
God
Individual
Others

People who have intellectual disabilities consider participation in a faith community as a preferred activity.[31] They benefit from their involvement in the church. The burden of religious communities is how to reach and include them. Individuals with intellectual disabilities bring challenges to faith communities such as their unconventional behavior. However, a relational spiritual formation model changes the focus from behaving in a socially acceptable manner to engaging with each other and God. What happens on a Sunday morning becomes secondary to being present before God and others. For example, focusing on the quality of the sermon or music is not as important as how the group accepts one another and expresses their relationship of acceptance and trust with each other and God.

Disability Ministry

While there is a connection between ministry with people with cognitive impairments and temporarily able-bodied people, certain elements are required for an effective ministry for people with intellectual disabilities. From a Disability Studies perspective, one theory applied in this guide is a social model of disability. A social model focuses on disability as an impairment only if the societal response excludes, separates, and does not allow full participation. For instance, a wheelchair is only an impairment if

---

[31] Victoria Slocum, "Recommendations for Including People with Intellectual Disabilities in Faith Communities," *Christian Education Journal* 13, no. 1 (2016): 124.

the environment does not permit a person to participate.[32] A medical model of disability contrasts starkly with a social model. The medical model views disability as something to heal. As a consequence, the primary issue of disability within the medical view becomes rehabilitation while the social model focuses on inclusion. The latter fits well within this guide's egalitarian foundation.

A central assumption for this guide is that those with intellectual disabilities need to function as co-laborers in ministry. Excluding people with cognitive impairments transforms them into objects of pity and subservient beings. Asking people with mental disabilities their preferences for spiritual growth is an important way for inclusion. Key themes for spiritual growth identified by individuals with intellectual disabilities are support, acceptance, and understanding.[33] Any plan for spiritual formation must consider these things while listening and working alongside all people in the ministry.

Leading a person with an intellectual disability in a Sinner's Prayer to begin their salvation journey is not necessary. Likewise, individuals with intellectual disabilities are not holy innocents who are incapable of sin and free from the need for salvation. People with cognitive

---

[32] John Swinton, "Who is the God We Worship? Theologies of Disability: Challenges and New Possibilities," *International Journal of Practical Theology* 14 (February 2011): 278.

[33] Richard Hobbs, Jennifer Fogo, and C. Elizabeth Bonham, "Individuals with Disabilities: Critical Factors that Facilitate Integration in Christian Religious Communities," *Journal of Rehabilitation* 82, no. 1 (2016): 40-41.

impairments are saved in the same way that anyone else is saved, through an on-going relationship with God and others in community. The challenge for faith communities is how to incorporate religious rituals for salvation, develop spiritual growth milestones, and communicate transformation in Heaven.

The main focus of salvation for people with intellectual disabilities needs to be starting and developing relationships with others. This approach focuses on salvation as a relationship that is upward to God and vertical toward others in the community.[34] Involving people with mental impairments in the life of the religious community connects them to God through participation and acceptance as a member of the community. Therefore, sharing the Gospel with someone who has an intellectual disability is not regurgitating a set of propositional truths but befriending them. Spiritual growth is not ensuring that a person with a cognitive impairment understands and accepts a particular theological position, but instead, spiritual growth occurs when the person with a disability is fully accepted and included in the religious life of the organization.

The caregiver or religious leader is the physical representative of God to the person with intellectual disabilities. Therefore, a strong, nurturing relationship with a caregiver or minister, communicates a solid relationship with God. A person with profound intellectual disabilities who is non-verbal and non-

---

[34] Tim Basselin, "Why Theology Needs Disability," *Theology Today* 68 (2011): 56.

ambulatory experiences God when he or she is accepted and loved by another human, who is made in God's image. The concept of salvation by grace through faith is reoriented from the mental agreement to truths to the experiential living. Salvation, grace, and faith are all applied to the interactions between the person with an intellectual disability, the community of faith, and God.

IQ is not representational of age and ability. Years of education, maturity, and life experience allow people with intellectual disabilities to gain skills and capabilities that are not usually recognized.[35] A support staff may talk to an individual with a cognitive impairment like a child through using a sweet, high-pitched voice. The same staff could also discount the person with an intellectual disability through denying personal choice because the person with a disability has an IQ similar to a child. Not recognizing that someone is an adult disrespects that person.

Individuals with intellectual disabilities should be able to outline their definition of quality of life. A person without a disability may describe quality of life as self-determination and mobility. The challenge with this definition is that a person with a disability may always have been non-ambulatory and dependent on others for daily needs. Those with profound intellectual and medical disabilities depend on others for

---

[35] Hefziba Lifshitz-Vahav, "Compensation Age Theory: Effect of Chronological Age on Individuals with Intellectual Disability," *Education and Training in Autism and Disabilities* 50, no. 2 (June 2015): 142.

daily living and quality of life.[36] The non-disabled person needs self-awareness to ensure that he or she is not imposing his or her views or standards onto the person with a profound or severe intellectual disability.

Pastoral Care Approach

The pastoral caregiver's purpose comprises of developing relationships and connecting others with the Divine. Building relationships with people who have profound disabilities involves a willingness to step outside of one's comfort zone and preferred methods of communication. Studies show that the defining characteristics which lead to positive relationships with people who have severe cognitive impairments are acceptance, celebration, trust, adjustment of communication style, mutual respect, reciprocity, and acknowledgment of individuality.[37]

In this context, the pastoral caregiver does not always deal with reality, nor does he try to find the objective truth. Instead, he enters the world of the other person to understand the individual's truth. A person with an intellectual disability who also has a psychiatric illness, or a severe communication issue, may be unable to express himself or herself in a logical manner.

---

[36] Juyoung Lee, "A Phenomenological Study of the Interpersonal Relationships Between Five Music Therapists and Adults with Profound Intellectual and Multiple Disabilities," *Qualitative Inquiries in Music Therapy* 9 (2014): 46.

[37] Hilary Johnson, et al, "A Model of Processes that Underpin Positive Relationships for Adults with Severe Intellectual Disability," *Journal of Intellectual & Developmental Disability* 37, no. 4 (December 2012): 325.

Stories and perceptions may vary considerably and include inaccurate information. However, classifying a person's beliefs as irrational or delusional before attending to his or her religious needs is ethically inappropriate.[38] The expression of an illogical, unrealistic story may contain an underlying pastoral need.

Identifying a covert spiritual need is hard. However, a pastoral assessment can occur through listening to how a person understands God, mortality, self, and vulnerability.[39] This kind of attentiveness assists the minister in better learning how to listen, love, and serve. If the individual and minister have different theological understandings, the cleric suspends his or her views to serve the individual best. The minister does not change personal beliefs; he uses the other person's belief system to provide healing.

A practical reality of my approach to ministry is the use of humor. Laughter bonds people and communicates profound truths. Merriment prevents burnout and being a court jester connects people to the King of Kings. Playfulness allows people to let their guard down while providing perspective on life. Four simple comedic types that work well in an environment with people who have intellectual disabilities are uncouthness, pranks, jokes, and banter.[40]

---

[38] Zehra Ersahin, "The Elephant in the Room: Implications of the on-going Conflict Between Religion and Science, and What Pluralism Offers Working with the (in) Visible," *Counseling Psychology Review* 28, no. 2 (June 2013): 43.

[39] Fredrick J. Streets, "Love: A Philosophy for Pastoral Care and Counseling," *Verbum et Ecclesia* 2, no. 35 (2014): 4.

[40] Johnson, et al., 329.

Ultimately, the minister must improvise and take what another person gives.

There is a major difference between laughing with and laughing at someone with an intellectual disability. Laughing at someone with an intellectual disability is never appropriate or helpful. However, you can laugh with someone who has a cognitive impairment about a situation. The minister can act foolishly and be the one who is laughed at, or he can provide levity to the situation through playfulness or humor.

There is a connection between humor and improvisation. One example of a small use of both is if a person with an intellectual disability pointed his index finger at you with his thumb in the air in the form of a gun. Does the pastoral caregiver ignore the attempted heist or the sheriff arresting the criminal? Instead, I propose that the pastoral caregiver immediately put his hands in the air and shout, "Don't shoot!" If the pastoral caregiver is shot, I recommend that he or she grab ahold of the wounded area and fall back. I have done this exact thing, many times in many different places. Sometimes it has happened to me on a Sunday morning while I am performing a ministerial task.

The silly banter and play is a sacramental ritual. The humor bonds the pastoral caregiver to the person with an intellectual disability, and it validates the humor and playfulness of the person with an intellectual disability. People like to feel important, and it feels good to have others laugh at your jokes. Scolding a person with, "We don't do that here," damages the relationship and misses an opportunity to join what God is doing. The minister does not have to be a comedic genius; he or she only needs to be open and willing to accept and laugh at what the other person is offering.

Relationships are primary to people who have intellectual disabilities. For example, they will not engage in religious services or events by themselves. People with intellectual disabilities may need additional supports to attend a service. One national study showed that only six percent of people with intellectual disabilities who attended congregational activities did so alone.[41] An invitation or a new program will not reach those who have intellectual disabilities. They need personal relationships to maintain involvement in the religious community. Friendship serves people with mental impairments as the best Gospel sermon.

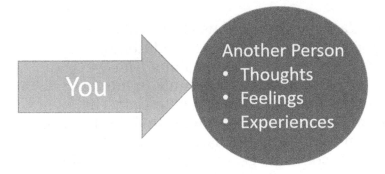

Empathy is the cornerstone of community, which drastically contrasts individualism—the

---

[41] Erik W. Carter, et al., "Congregational Participation of a National Sample of Adults with Intellectual and Developmental Disabilities," *Intellectual and Developmental Disabilities* 53 (2015): 391.

dominate trait in our culture. Empathy allows a person to experience the life of another.[42] The duty of a minister is to join people and connect them to the Almighty. The interdependence between people and God constitutes a primary part of the spiritual formation process. Instead of living the Golden Rule, the empathetic person interacts with the other person as the other person wants. Treating the other individual based on his or her personal preference is particularly important in pastoral care relationships to those who have intellectual disabilities. The pastoral caregiver may not be that excited about birthdays or an incidental circumstance. However, for the person with cognitive impairments, the seemingly small event may be a vital life experience. In this pastoral care approach, the minister celebrates with others when they rejoice.

Music and Worship

While relational connections are the lifeline, religious services function as conduits to establish and mature relationships. These events create opportunities for all people to interact, meet each other, and connect with God. The freedom that people with intellectual disabilities exhibit in fully being themselves is an act of worship. If someone gets up during the worship singing or sermon, it is not a sign of disrespect. The person is just being him or herself and feels the liberty to act accordingly. If a person with an

---

[42] Andrew Root, *The Relational Pastor: Sharing Christ by Sharing Ourselves* (Downers Grove: InterVarsity Press, 2013), 92.

intellectual disability speaks out of turn in a worship service, that is an opportunity for him or her to receive validation, not rebuke. The person with a cognitive impairment often does not know or understand social cues. Accepting what they say and responding with a "thank you" communicates God's love and approval.

In the worship setting, the leader comes alongside the congregation to connect them with God. During worship with people who have intellectual disabilities, the pastoral emphasis is not on leading in a traditional sense. The primary pastoral task in public worship is stimulating ironic imagination: life through death, the blessed poor, and boastful sufferers. Irony in this context accepts the tension that is inherent in reality.[43] The pastoral task is not to solve the tension of the worshipers, but instead, the minister invites the congregants into the sacred space of tension.

Ironic imagination can be stimulated at worship services. For example, the leader becomes a fellow worshipper instead of a specialist. Although the minister is leading, has a special calling, and possess unique educational experiences, he or she is also a learner and a member of the religious community. Therefore, the minister empties himself or herself, helps the congregation theologically reflect, and facilitates self-expression towards God through the service. Spending a religious service trying to contain, control, and teach those with

---

[43] Neil Pembroke, "Witness to Hope in the Christian Community Through Irony," *Pastoral Psychology* 58 (2009): 433-434.

intellectual disabilities the societal expectations hampers their worship, denies their self-expression toward God, and limits what the minister can learn.

How the minister and congregation respond to an interruption or outburst of someone who has an intellectual disability communicates that religious community's priorities. The person with an intellectual disability is not trying to maliciously cause problems in the service. He or she is responding to God and others in the best way that they can.

The flow chart offers an alternate view of how to handle and view interruptions at the worship service. Interruptions are an opportunity for everyone in your congregation to learn and grow.

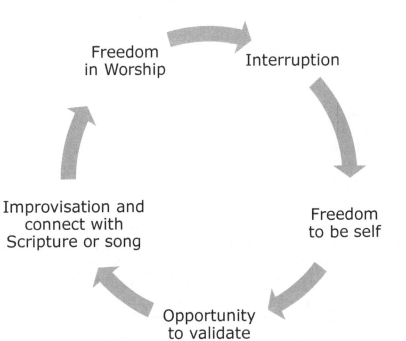

Freedom
in Worship

Interruption

Freedom
to be self

Opportunity
to validate

Improvisation and
connect with
Scripture or song

Even if the congregation desires to eventually lead the person with a cognitive impairment to observe a more structured and silent service, the outburst can still be handled with grace and validation. Also, setting guidelines and letting the person be involved before or after the service can help. That way, the person with a cognitive impairment can understand that he or she helped out with the service and now it is someone else's turn.

Music offers one of the most effective ways to communicate and join with people who have intellectual disabilities. Individuals with extreme cognitive disabilities can use music as their primary connection with others.[44] Worship connects people to God while the music provides a link between each person in the community. Allowing the person with an intellectual disability as much choice as possible with the songs or singing communicates love and openness.

One way to offer choice is through developing a song choice book. All a person needs is a binder, paper, a printer that will allow them to print images related to the songs, and Velcro. The minister brings the Song Choice Book to the individual who then can pick out a song and pull it out of the book. Even if a person is non-verbal with profound disabilities, the minister can choose two songs and hold them in front of the individual. The pastoral caregiver can ask them which song and judge their decision through eye movement or level of excitement. After time

---

[44] Kenneth Aigen, "A Critique of Evidence-Based Practice in Music Therapy," *Music Therapy Perspectives* 33, no.1 (2015): 17.

passes, the minister will know the songs that the non-verbal person prefers.

Historically, music is used for the benefit of people with cognitive impairments. Employing music for individuals who have intellectual disabilities is rooted in behavioral psychology as it produces stimulation and reinforcement.[45] Having a worship service where the majority of the time is spent with music nourishes those with intellectual disabilities. If possible, letting the individual choose and lead the style and genre of music validates them as a person. Receiving affirmation in some way during a worship service could be one of the few times that someone celebrates the individual's contribution.

I understand that some churches or organizations will be limited to what they are able to do during a worship service. However, I would like to offer an example of my setting that may encourage creative thinking. One thing that we do is a song practice before the actual worship service. During the song practice, the individuals usually bring CD's or choose secular songs to sing. Even though the songs may be classified as country music or pop, it can still be a worshipful experience. The individual picks the song, sings to the best of his or her ability, and then everyone celebrates with him or her. It is worship because the individual is offering the best that he or she can in the house of God. It

---

[45] Jane V. Riddoch and Russell F. Waugh, "Teaching Students with Severe Intellectual Disabilities Non-Representational Art Using a New Pictorial and Music Programme," *Journal of Intellectual & Developmental Disability* 28, no.2 (June 2003): 146.

also validates his or her contribution, and that person leaves feeling very special.

There was one time when an individual brought a CD and told us which number he wanted to sing. He did not know the words, but that did not keep him from belting out sounds that followed the tune. During the song, he motioned for me to join him on stage. I stood by him, I leaned in next to him, and we both belted out the sounds of the song. This person taught me how to empty out myself and ego to join another person during their special moment. When we are working with those who have intellectual disabilities, we need to ask ourselves are we more concerned about what others may say or think about us or are we seeking God's heart. Emptying oneself out can be embarrassing, but a staunch and stubborn refusal speaks more about our heart than our willingness to be different for the sake of Christ and others.

For people who have cognitive impairments, music diminishes undesirable conduct and helps them deal with anxiety through a positive channel.[46] In my experience, people with intellectual disabilities have enjoyed the chapel services and specifically the music without behavioral challenges. Some of the people who exhibit consistent physical, aggressive behavior towards others do not show signs of aggression during the chapel services. The religious services

---

[46] Jeff Hooper, et al., "The Practical Implications of Comparing How Adults with and without Intellectual Disability Respond to Music," *British Journal of Learning Disabilities* 39 (2010): 27.

provide opportunities for affirmation and validation. The environment of the worship service and the music contributes to the lessening of these difficult behaviors.

In addition to music, Scripture and prayer are two other essential elements that can be included in worship. One way that I include prayer is through giving each individual an opportunity to pray. Sometimes the prayers can be quite unique. Some people feel the need to correct the prayers and theology of others. Instead, it is best to affirm those with an intellectual disability in any way possible. To ask someone for something, like a prayer, and then reject what they offer, through correcting, ensures that they will be reluctant to be themselves and vulnerable again.

Some of the people with intellectual disabilities are non-verbal. For these situations, we take a communication device with a pre-recorded prayer on it. I always ask the person if they would like to pray and after I attentively listen to their body language and expressions, I will either give them the opportunity to touch the prayer button, or I will gently push the button on their hand. The prayer is always tied to the Scripture reading for the day. However, utilizing the principles above of improvisation, sometimes a person may give you something unexpected. I had a non-verbal person with severe intellectual and physical disabilities provide a grunt when I asked for a prayer. I affirmed him and said, "That's a good prayer, thank you."

Generally, the sermons are very short—five minutes at the most. Typically, I use the lectionary to help with the Scripture selection. The audiences' level of disability impacts the message. Sometimes I speak more to the support staff in a pastoral care approach. I may include the names of the people in the audience. If they interrupt me, I listen and try to reincorporate what they offered in the message.

The primary consideration is that sermons and lesson plans are different from other forms of church ministry. The purpose of the sermon is not to transmit information, but rather, build relationships. When the minister preaches, he or she cultivates a relationship with the congregation. As the horizontal relationship between clergy and parishioners matures, the vertical relationship with God and the congregation develops.

When the main function is to transmit knowledge, then the minister becomes frustrated with interruption or wonders if the parishioners "got it." In a relational approach, the ability for the people to receive a new truth or correct wrong beliefs is inconsequently. Relational sermons provide an opportunity for the minister and the participants to engage with one another in a dialogue with one another and God. This takes the pressure off of the minister; spiritual education first occurs through being present and available to the people.

The last thing that I do with the Bible is utilize it as a symbol of God's love and communication. Before I speak for the Sunday Chapel Service, I will hold up the Bible and ask, "What is this?" People will yell back, "The Bible!" as they hold up their personal Bibles. I tell them, "That's right!

It's God's special book that tells us how much he loves us and how to live." Since I do this with the Bible, sometimes the same people want a new Bible every time they come to Chapel; I always give them one. The people know and I affirm that the Bible is unique and represents God's closeness and care.

While I provided some specific examples, they are not intended to serve as the only way. My hope is that the things I have done will spur on your imagination as you faithful serve at your place of ministry. A relational spiritual formation model is the best method to serve people who have cognitive impairments. The main emphasis of pastoral care to people with intellectual disabilities involves love, patience, flexibility, and empathy. Lastly, music and worship serve as the primary platform for a relational spiritual formation plan.

Evaluating Your Ministry

This evaluation section is not intended to be critical of your hard work. You are already doing a great job. How do I know that? Because first of all you show up to your ministry faithfully. As we learned earlier in this guide, presence is the central part of relationships and spiritual formation. Your presence in your place of ministry speaks volumes, and it is the best, and sometimes the only thing you have to offer. Keep showing up and continue engaging people and God.

Second, you are doing a good job because you are reading this guide. People do not learn things they are not interested in improving. Your heart of reading and engaging in this handbook is hard work. Individuals who are arrogant, lazy, and apathetic do not have an interest in growing. The fact that you are in section three of this guide shows your commitment to the people you minister alongside and serve. Continue to learn, grow, read, and join in the community knowing that faithfully serving and offering yourself to others is enough.

There are two areas of evaluation. The "Main Areas for Evaluation of Ministry"[47] provides six questions that cover overarching themes for the purpose and scope of ministry. The second area, "Evaluation of Spiritual Formation Guide for Worship Services,"[48] offers six questions where the minister and the other staff can measure the effectiveness of the religious service. For maximum usefulness, it is best to have multiple people complete this questionnaire to provide a whole picture. The first area serves as a game plan for the religious service while the second area seeks to measure how the minister and congregants respond to that game plan. The rationale for each question is below so that you can understand their purpose and design.

Main Areas for Evaluation of Ministry

The six questions in this section are designed to provide an overall assessment of ministry. The below questions engage in the top areas of ministry in an institutional setting for people with intellectual disabilities. These six reflective questions are primarily for the minister to ask himself or herself. The chief topics include a

---

[47] Appendix A.
[48] Appendix B.

connection with the Divine, community, inclusivity, coping, personal choice, and mutual ministry. These six elements are foundational for a ministry with people who have intellectual disabilities.

Does the ministry help people feel connected with the Divine?

A primary function of my work as a chaplain in a pluralistic setting is connecting people with the Divine. Sometimes this comes in times of loss and trauma. On other occasions, I connect them with the Divine through offering my presence, as one who is of God and sent by God. A significant role of the religious service is then helping people unite with the Divine. The minister wants people leaving the worship service having encountered the living God.

Does the ministry connect people with each other?

While connecting upwards to God, it is equally important for people to connect outwards with each other. If only connecting to God were important, people could stay at home and worship, and there would be no need for the church. We need other people for spiritual growth. The whole Church matures through everyone giving and receiving. In a recent study, individuals with intellectual disabilities identified community, beliefs, rituals, and practices as key elements that define religion.[49] The participants of the worship service should

---

[49] Hobbs, et al., 37.

experience a connection with the worshipping community locally and universally. In addition to experiencing fellowship, the minister can emphasize and reflect about the link between beliefs, rituals, and practices.

Is the ministry honoring and does it bring dignity to people who have intellectual disabilities?

Ministry needs to be God-honoring. The creative and redemptive power of God results in celebration and life. Part of giving glory to God is offering dignity to people who have intellectual disabilities. People with mental disabilities are made in the image of God, and part of that is participating in relationships of mutual responsiveness.[50] Since individuals with intellectual disabilities are a vulnerable population, extra measures need to occur to ensure they are not being oppressed or neglected.

Does the ministry help people cope?

Studies show that spirituality impacts three areas: mortality, coping, and recovery.[51] When I talk to other disciplines at my facility, they see a primary value of chaplaincy as helping people cope. I think they are right. Spiritually is not in competition with other disciplines. There is a role for the physical, the psychological, and the spiritual in holistic care. A strength of spirituality is that it offers transcendence in ways that the physical and mental cannot. A

---

[50] Haslam, 104.
[51] Anita Goh, et al., "Pastoral Care in Old Age Psychiatry: Addressing the Spiritual Needs of Inpatients in an Acute Aged Mental Health Unit," *Asia-Pacific Psychiatry* 6 (2015): 128.

primary function in ministry, therefore, helps people look beyond themselves to cope.

Does the ministry and worship services allow for personal choice?

Many people with intellectual disabilities are without choice in their life. Caregivers and staff tell them what, when, and how to do something. A ministry that does not infantilize people with intellectual disabilities provides choices. Sometimes the choice that a person with a cognitive impairment makes may be different than a traditional option. Instead of scolding that person or trying to get them to confine to norms, the minister and others in the congregation can all experience growth through this improvisation of grace.

Does the ministry recognize the gifts, talents, and contributions of everyone?

A significant tenant of this guide is that the Body of Christ requires the participation of everyone. This criterion of evaluation recognizes the contributions of all people. If individuals who have intellectual disabilities are only the recipients of ministry, then the caregivers, clergy, and the rest of the community of faith miss out. People with mental disabilities have substantial gifts to offer their religious communities, and ministry leaders can recognize, shape, and assist others in reflecting on disability and the gift people with intellectual disability offer.

While the above evaluation questions focus
broadly, the below six questions hone into
observable details and feelings during the
worship service. These questions serve as a
guide for the minister during and after the
service. While the first six questions are for the
minister to ask himself or herself, these next six
questions are for the minister to ask about the
congregation. It is a way to check-in and reframe
what is happening. Personally, I have worked
hard to prepare chapel services only to abandon
everything that I planned. However, after further
reflection and engagement in questions like the
ones below, I reframed my previous negative
assessment of the situation. Just because things
went differently does not mean that they are not
right. Sometimes having something tangible to
point to in the service can allow the minister to
feel refreshed and reenergized.

*Examine the thoughts, feelings, and observations
of the participants such as body language, verbal
cues, and facial expressions.*

One of the best things the minister can do is
observe. Even when the participants cannot
verbalize their experiences, they will tell how the
service is impacting them in other ways. What
are the congregants doing throughout the
service? Is he or she clapping, smiling, or actively
engaged? Another indicator is how the person
with an intellectual disability reacts around the
minister. Does the parishioner smile when the
minister touches his or her shoulder or when the

minister speaks? Is the congregant overjoyed to share about a recent experience, what he or she loves, or an upcoming exciting event? These questions help the minister gauge the personal impact of the person with an intellectual disability and the development of relationships.

The people willingly participated and engaged in the service.

This question starts with five options, from Strongly Agree to Strongly Disagree, along with an Additional Comments section. This question will help the minister measure three things. First, it will show the inclusivity of the religious service. If congregants are not actively involved, then the service is probably not designed with them in mind. However, if they are participating, it will show that the service at least has them as a priority. Second, the level of participation of people with intellectual disabilities will demonstrate their interest in the service. If they are bored and unengaged, they will just be sitting on the peripheral not trying to talk or participate. A parishioner saying something in the middle of a sermon is not a bad thing. This interruption shows the person's interest and willingness to be part of the worship service. Instead of viewing these as disruptions and antisocial behaviors, the minister can reframe the experience as the person fully expressing himself or herself in the presence of God. Lastly, individuals with intellectual disabilities usually need sensory awareness and close human contact for spiritual growth.[52] If the individuals are actively and willingly participating, they are perhaps experiencing sensory and relational engagement.

Do the behaviors of the participants demonstrate that they are engaged spiritually? More specifically, are the people showing joyous expressions, do they exhibit a willingness to confide or engage with the minister, and are the people free to express themselves through worship?

This question starts with five options, from Strongly Agree to Strongly Disagree, along with an Additional Comments section. The facility where I work emphasizes Positive Behavior Support Plans and also utilizes Board Certified Behavioral Analysts (BCBA). These professionals clearly contribute to the individual's life, and they help the institution. However, the chaplain is not a BCBA, and a lot of what the minister deals with is unmeasurable and emotional. Out of the cognitive, emotional, and behavioral elements of humanity, behavior is the only one that is observable.[53] There is much the minister can learn from these professionals as they work together. It is a challenge to measure the mystical. Spirituality is unmeasurable, but the minister can see the effects of a spiritual life and the worship. The Apostle Paul defines this as the Fruit of the Spirit: love, joy, peace, patience,

---

[52] John Baker, "Spiritual Education in the Special School Setting for Pupils with Learning Difficulties/Disabilities," *International Journal of Children's Spirituality* 17, no. 2 (May 2012): 161-162.

[53] Aigen, 13.

kindness, goodness, faithfulness, gentleness, and self-control.[54]

What is the level of involvement or engagement of the support staff? Are the support staff assisting? Do they seem engaged through body affect?

This question starts with five options, from Strongly Agree to Strongly Disagree, along with an Additional Comments section. A forgotten element in institutional life is the support staff who help the individuals with their functioning. When I first got to my facility, I developed the mission statement, "We exist to provide pastoral care and counseling to the residents, staff, and family members." Previously, it seemed like the employees were left out. Neglecting the caregivers translate into the lackluster treatment of those they serve. Ideally the better the staff are treated, the better care they can offer to others. Measuring the staff's level of involvement with the religious service will indicate if the employees are being fed spiritually and it will help the experience of those with intellectual disabilities. If the staff are humdrum, others will feed off of the negative energy.

While staff involvement is crucial, do not place too much emphasis on it. There are many reasons why a staff member may not want to participate in the chapel service. Staff may not know how to help. Most staff are conditioned to think that church is a place where people sit and listen. Second, staff may not want to participate because of a previous spiritual wounding or

---

[54] Galatians 5:22-23.

deeply held convictions. A particular staff may have a different religious belief than what is being taught in the service.

What is the attitude and expression of the participants before and after the service?
This question is open-ended and designed to create reflection and dialogue. I always feel tempted by television commercials that provide before and after pictures. Whether it is weight loss, home repair, or a cleaning product, my first instinct is to imagine how the product would impact my life. The before and after effect is powerful. Likewise, measuring the before and after effect of the participants can provide perspective and encouragement. Did people come to the service down, but leave with a sense of connection with God? Did relationships start off tense, but grow by the end of the service? These are signs that something special occurred. There is a transformational effect that takes place through chaplaincy. At first, I fought against this idea. However, a friend pushed me and asked, "Why are you there then? What difference do you make?" I started to reframe past ideas of transformation and recognize little, significant changes. Look out for these changes in your ministry.

How does the minister feel before and after the service?
This question is open-ended and designed to create reflection and dialogue. The last question deals with the minister's ability to be self-aware and cultural reflective. How did the minister feel

before and after the service? What are the practices, social interactions, and shared experiences of the religious service?[55] The minister evaluates himself or herself while also assessing practices, interactions, and meanings as the individuals attend chapel and go about their daily lives. When the minister is not aware of his or her feelings before the service, it will impact the quality of the service and the minister's outlook of the events. There have been times when stress or sadness before the service dominated my ability to engage and observe the events. I am not advocating that a minister put on a façade. Instead, recognizing how one feels and any personal bias is imperative. The intent of having this question last is that answering the other issues may help the minister identify covert feelings and dynamics that happened throughout the service. Whatever dominant issue or theme that the minister recognizes for the participants, it is probably an indicator of projection of personal and unconscious feelings by the minister.

---

[55] Robert Aronowitz, et al., "Cultural Reflexivity in Health Research and Practice," *American Journal of Public Health* 105, no. 53 (2015): 404.

My Project as an Example

Below you will find eight examples of applying the teachings from this guide, which comes for my Doctor of Ministry Project.[56] The context for the services is my ministry as a chaplain at a large residential facility for adults with intellectual disabilities. The chapel services are over a four week period and divided into a total of eight chapel services. Each of the four weeks is similar. Two services were held a week, starting with the existing chapel service and concluding with a new chapel worship service. Each section presents the necessary information about a particular worship service, field notes concerning the sermon and reflection, and the completed questionnaires by the chapel team.[57] The examples from the services are not to serve as a template for ministry. Instead, I encourage the reader to see how I incorporated the approaches in the spiritual formation guide for these particular situations. Then, I hope the readers will think about how they can do the same in their context.

First Existing Chapel Service

The Scripture was Luke 23:39–43, which relates to the two thieves on the cross with Jesus. The service's central message was that Jesus' forgiveness passes expectations. A total of 33 residents, seven support staff members, four

---

[56] Wesley D. Cohoon, "A Relationship-Based Spiritual Formation Plan for Adults with Intellectual Disabilities," Doctor of Ministry Project, Logsdon Seminary, Abilene, 2017.

[57] The evaluation for the chapel service is the "Evaluation of Spiritual Formation Guide at the Worship Services" found in Appendix B.

chapel employees, and one family member of a resident were in attendance. The service lasted one hour and fifteen minutes, with an hour of fellowship time held before the service.

To start the sermon, I asked the residents what was happening on Thursday. Several of the residents yelled out "Thanksgiving!" I affirmed them and asked about their Thanksgiving plans. From the pulpit, I called on several people; some just yelled out their favorite foods. I shifted gears and said, "We eat all of that on Thanksgiving because we are thankful. But there is even more to be thankful about than the food we eat."

Then I transitioned by holding up the Bible and telling the audience, "Today we are going to read a story from this." I asked the congregants what was in my hand, and several of them yelled out "The Bible!" Many people started holding up or pointing to their Bibles. I affirmed them, noting, "The Bible is God's special book that tells us how much God loves us and how to live. Today we are going to read what God tells us to be thankful about."

One of the individuals on the stage then started yelling, "I'll do it! I'll do it!" I called her by name and asked if she wanted to help, even though she is not able to read. The individual said yes, so I gave her the microphone and read the passage out loud for the individual to repeat. When we were done with the passage, the individual started talking about a support staff in the audience who she liked. I let her finish, and then the individual returned the microphone to me. I thanked the individual and then told everyone else, "*Betty*[58] was telling us about the two thieves who were on the cross next to Jesus. One of them was making fun of Jesus, while the other one asked for forgiveness. And Jesus forgave the one who asked for forgiveness and told him that they would be in heaven together. You see, Jesus' forgiveness goes beyond what we expect. So this Thanksgiving, we can be thankful for Jesus' forgiveness."

At that point, a different individual arose and approached the pulpit. She asked, "What about marriage?" The individual told me that she loved another person and wanted to marry him. She then asked, "How can I marry him?" I responded, "That is a good point. What I hear *Samantha* talk about is that this Thanksgiving she can be thankful for people we love. You are thankful for him, right?" The resident smiled and replied yes, and I affirmed her.

People in the audience then started talking about people they were thankful for and loved. I let everyone share. At the very end, one of the individuals had his hand up very high and straight. I told everyone that he was going to let the person with his hand eagerly up say the final word before the prayer. That individual said, "I'm going to eat pumpkin pie!" I exclaimed, "Yes, me too! And that gets us back to Thanksgiving. We are thankful for the people we love, we are thankful for God, we are thankful

---

[58] All of the residents' names used in this section are pseudonyms.

for Jesus' forgiveness, and we are going to get together this Thursday and celebrate that thankfulness through eating pumpkin pie, pecan pie, turkey, and all of our favorite foods! Now let us pray." The prayer was followed by the closing song, after which the people arose and left.

Reflective Entry about the First Existing Service

A relational spiritual formation paradigm is not anti-intellectual. The sermon had a lesson for the residents, and they seemed to grasp it. The residents moved from associating Thanksgiving with food to associating it with more substantial things, such as being thankful for people.

Completed Questionnaires from the First Existing Service

The first question, which is open-ended, allows the respondent to observe the participants' body language, verbal cues, and facial expressions. To classify and evaluate the responses to the open-ended questions, I categorized them as *positive*, *negative*, or *neutral*. For the first question, the first two respondents offered *positive* statements, while the third respondent provided a *neutral* observation. The second respondent observed two residents who typically have challenging behaviors express a desire to sing additional songs. When I explained that everyone needed a chance to sing first, the residents seemed okay with the response. The second respondent felt that being told they could not sing another song would normally result in a behavioral challenge by the residents. However, the second respondent attributed the residents' calm response to the residents being in the chapel and the previous relationship that the chaplain established with them. The third respondent made *neutral* observations about the residents, but he did include a story of a resident's mother crying when her son sang at the service.

Question two through four utilize a five-point Likert-scale (ranging from *strongly agree* to *strongly disagree*). Question two asks about the residents' participation in the chapel service, and all three respondents *strongly agreed* that the residents were engaged in the service. Question three asks if the residents demonstrated certain behaviors that showed their spiritual engagement. Two respondents *strongly agreed* and the third respondent *agreed* that the residents exhibited behaviors that showed spiritual engagement. Question four asks about the staff's involvement in the service. Two respondents *agreed* that staff members were involved and the third respondent both *agreed* and *disagreed* with the statement (as he noticed that some staff members were involved while others were not).

Question five is an open-ended question that deals with the participants' attitudes before and after the service. All three respondents made *positive* statements regarding the attitudes of the residents. One respondent noticed that a particular resident did not want to leave after the service was over. Another respondent characterized the residents as happy, excited, and joyful before and after the service. The last respondent reported that the residents were social and talkative.

Question six asks how the respondents felt before and after the service. The second respondent felt happy and encouraged at both junctures. Respondents One and Three expressed *negative* responses concerning how they felt before the service. Respondent Three was tired both before and after the service and reported that he was pensive and excited about an unread email. Respondent One felt nervous before the service but excited after.

First New Chapel Service

The first new chapel service took place on Monday, November 21, 2016. The Scripture was Luke 23:39-43, which relates to the two thieves on the cross with Jesus. The sermon's main message was that Thanksgiving is coming, so we can be thankful like the second criminal on the cross. A total of 14 residents, three support staff members, and three chapel employees were in attendance. The service lasted 30 minutes.

Sermon Field Notes for the First New Service

I anticipated that some residents who attended the Sunday service may also attend the Monday service. Therefore, I planned to change the service a little while keeping the Thanksgiving theme. I decided to use the second criminal as an example of a thankful attitude, the first criminal as an example of how not to respond, and Jesus as an example of God's love and forgiveness.

When I read the verse that details what the second criminal said, one of the residents intervened, "He said, 'forgive me'!" I told the resident, "That's right! He did! The second criminal said, 'Forgive me and please remember me when you come into your kingdom.' " My impromptu paraphrase of Luke 23:40-42 was intended to validate the resident and incorporate the resident into the story. I also felt like the resident was right—the thief essentially did say, "Forgive me." It was not a time for correction, but an opportunity for listening. At the end of the service, one of the residents approached me. She told me about people she loved and that she was looking forward to Thanksgiving. As I listened to her, the resident became excited, and I mirrored the excitement.

Reflective Entry about the First New Service
Only one staff member at the workshop was expecting the chaplaincy team. Previously, I spoke with one workshop staff member and the workshop supervisors to schedule the service. The supervisors had told me that they would inform the other workshop staff. I felt a little frustrated, as communication problems can be common at my facility. The workshop staff explained to the other staff what the chaplaincy team was doing and welcomed their participation and input. The staff member who was most involved with the chapel service was the one who did not expect the chapel service. It seems that the chaplaincy team's previous relationship with the staff and residents helped

the service, which is briefer than on Sunday and does not include fellowship time.

Respondents One and Three provided *negative* statements regarding question one, which deals with the participants' body language, verbal cues, and facial expressions. Respondent One pointed out that the workshop staff were not expecting the chaplaincy team. Respondents One and Three observed several residents who seemed disengaged. Respondent Two offered a *positive* statement regarding question one, as he noticed a resident who was happy to see the chaplaincy team and saw some residents laughing during the service.

In relation to questions two through four (which use the Likert-scale), respondents One and Three *agreed* regarding the residents' participation in the service. Respondent Two *strongly agreed* that the residents fully participated. Respondents One and Two *strongly agreed* that the residents exhibited behaviors that showed spiritual engagement, while Respondent Three *agreed*. Finally, all respondents *agreed* that the support staff were involved in the chapel service.

In question five, all three respondents provided *positive* statements regarding participants' attitudes before and after the service. Respondent One reported that the residents were surprised and happy to see the chaplaincy team. Respondent Two felt like the residents enjoyed singing during chapel.

Respondent Three wrote that many residents appeared to have a flat attitude before the service but were smiling and talkative after it.

Regarding question six, Respondents One and Two provided *positive* statements about their own feelings before and after the service. Respondent One enjoyed the chaplaincy team's fellowship time on the way to the service. Respondent Two had a good time and thought this area will request a chapel service every week. Respondent Three provided a *negative* statement about his feelings before the service, as he felt nervous (which he attributed to it being a new service); he reported feeling relief once it was over.

Second Existing Chapel Service

The second chapel worship service occurred on Sunday, November 27, 2016. The Scripture was Romans 13:10, "Love does no harm to its neighbor. Therefore, love is the fulfillment of the law." The sermon's central message was that love is God's number one rule. A total of 24 individuals, seven support staff members, and three ministerial employees were in attendance. The service lasted approximately one hour.

Sermon Field Notes for the Second Existing Service

When I stepped into the pulpit, I held the Bible up and asked, "What is this?" Several residents yelled out "The Bible!" as they held or pointed to their Bibles. I affirmed them and told them, "The Bible is God's special book that tells us how much he loves us and how to live." At this point a resident sitting on the stage stood up and tapped me on the shoulder. He told me that his mother was in the hospital. I informed the resident that I would pray for his mother, put my arm on the resident's shoulder, and proceeded to tell the group about the individual's mother. I also said, "That is another thing about the Bible. When we are sad, sick, or alone, we can have the Bible with us and know that God cares for us."

The music therapist had already read Romans 13:10 for one of the songs, so I acknowledged that this verse had been read earlier in the service. I informed the congregants that they would listen to it again and then discuss it. After re-reading the verse, I told the residents that the number one thing that God cared about was love. A few residents interrupted me to share about various things. I listened and tied what they were saying to love. As I talked about love, I used a few positive examples from the residents concerning how they show love to other people. I called the residents out by name and affirmed how they showed love to another person or what they did.

In the end, I offered a prayer. The final song is always "God Be with You," and the residents usually remain seated until it is played. Once the song starts, they get out of their chairs and start to leave. The music therapist had a situation to handle, so he was not in the front of the room to play the song. The chaplaincy assistant and I were not expecting this but led the congregation in an a cappella version of "God Be with You." The music therapist was eventually able to run to the front and start playing the song on the keyboard.

The relational approach seems easier when the group is smaller and an existing relationship exists. Having a history and a relationship outside of a chapel service provides an opportunity to connect the message and pastoral care back to each resident in a meaningful manner. The improvisation with the closing song at the end of the service was important, as it reminded me of the need to put aside pretense to offer what is needed. My ability to sing did not matter in that moment. Risking vulnerability is a necessary part of improvisation.

All three respondents provided *positive* statements regarding the residents' body language, verbal cues, and facial expressions. Respondent One noticed that Resident A made Resident B visibly angry. Resident A then went over to Resident B to apologize and shake his hand. Resident B accepted the handshake and the situation was over. Respondent Two observed several expressions of love at the service. Resident C discovered that it had been Respondent Two's birthday over the weekend and sang to him. Respondent Two also noticed that Resident D let Resident E (who has a physical disability and is sometimes difficult to sit next to) sit by him. Respondent Three wrote about the song requests and how the music therapist changed the lyrics to fit the residents' personality and preferences.

All three respondents *strongly agreed* about the residents' level of participation in the service. Respondents One and Two *strongly agreed* that the residents exhibited behaviors that expressed spiritual engagement, whereas Respondent Three only *agreed*. Respondent One *strongly agreed* that the support staff participated in the service. In the comments section, Respondent One provided a few examples of staff involvement. One staff member asked Respondent One to print pictures for the residents to color after the service. Another staff member asked for a Bible for a resident who does not verbalize many requests and whose Bible is torn. Lastly, a staff member stayed to help re-organize the room after the chapel service. Respondents Two and Three *agreed* that staff members were involved in the chapel service.

All three respondents provided *positive* remarks concerning the participants' attitudes before and after the service. Respondent Two felt that the residents were excited at both points. One resident approached Respondent Three from behind, put his hands over the respondent's eyes, and announced "I'm back!" Another resident positively shared about relationship issues with Respondent Three, and many residents spoke positively about the upcoming Christmas pageant.

Respondent Two felt happy and connected both before and after the service. Respondents

One and Three reporting having *negative* feelings before the service and *positive* feelings afterward. Respondent One felt pressured before the service and energized after. Respondent Three felt drowsy and nervous before the service but refreshed by the end.

Second New Worship Service

The second new chapel service was held on Monday, November 28, 2016. The Scripture was Romans 13:10, "Love does no harm to its neighbor. Therefore, love is the fulfillment of the law." The sermon's central message was that love helps people. A total of 11 individuals, three support staff members, and three ministerial employees were present. The service lasted approximately 30 minutes.

Sermon Field Notes for the Second New Service

The title of the message was "Love helps people." The music therapist introduced me by saying that I was going to talk about a Bible verse that is about love. I thanked the music therapist and playfully said that many verses in the Bible are about love. Then I read Romans 13:10 to the congregants, noting, "This verse tells us that love helps people." I stated that people can help in several ways, but the main way is through loving others. When someone is nice, that person loves others. I talked about friendship and how easy it is to be someone's friend and love him or her.

Some of the residents spoke up about helping people and being a friend. I affirmed them and said they are doing a good job of loving people, which is what God wants. I ended the message by announcing that the music therapist would sing a final song and that the chaplaincy team would be back the next week.

Reflective Entry about the Second New Service

In stark comparison to the previous week, the support staff seemed overjoyed to see the chaplaincy team. Developing a relationship with staff members and providing them some relief offers pastoral care to both them and the residents. I spent most of the service writing out the dates and times of the four Christmas pageant performances. After I responded to one resident's request for this information, residents kept coming to ask for their own copy. I viewed this as an act of pastoral care and relationship building with the residents. The residents associate the Christmas pageant with Jesus, and they associate the chaplain with the Christmas pageant. My act of writing that information out for them thus demonstrated care and interest from God.

Completed Questionnaires from the Second New Service

All three respondents provided *positive* remarks and observations about the residents' body language, verbal cues, and facial expressions. Respondent One noted that the residents appeared happy, requested songs without prompting, and verbalized prayers for themselves and each other. Respondent Two observed that several residents gave the chaplaincy team hugs and immediately communicated their song preferences through sign language. Respondent Three commented that a resident who appeared disengaged during the last service was engaged, smiling, and involved in the service.

For the three Likert-scale questions, Respondents One and Two *strongly agreed* that the residents participated fully in the service, while Respondent Three *agreed*. Respondents One and Two also *strongly agreed* that the residents showed spiritual engagement through their attitudes, whereas Respondent Three *agreed*. Respondent Two reported that this new service reminded him of the existing service in that the residents talk to the ministers about life and the ministers provide pastoral support and attentive listening. Respondent One *strongly agreed* and Respondents Two and Three *agreed* that the support staff were involved. Respondent Three reported that some of the staff clapped with the songs and encouraged the residents to do the same, and another staff member came from her workshop room to assist with a resident. Respondent One reported *positive* support staff interactions, including one staff member initiating a joke in the service, another clapping, and a third personally disclosing to the minister about his life at the end of the service.

All three respondents positively commented about the participants' attitudes before and after the service. Respondent One mentioned that the staff and residents were happy to see and thanked the chaplaincy team. Respondent Two commented that the residents seemed to enjoy selecting songs for worship and that most of them showed joyful attitudes throughout the service. Respondent Three noted that many residents were excited about the upcoming Christmas pageant.

All three respondents also expressed *positive* feedback regarding how they felt before and after the service. Respondent Two reported that he felt happy and connected before and after the service, adding that the residents seemed appreciative for the service. He noted that he felt the service meant a great deal to the residents, and he felt the residents' expressed a desire for the next one. A connection between vocational fulfillment and the *positive* responses of Respondent Two therefore seems to exist. Respondent Three felt more confident in this service than he did in the last new service. After the service, Respondent Two felt that many more residents were involved than in the previous week's service.

Third Existing Worship Service

The third existing worship service occurred on Sunday, December 4, 2016. The Scripture was Romans 15:1–3a, "We who are strong ought to bear with the failings of the weak and not to please ourselves. Each of us should please his neighbor for his good, to build him up. For even Christ did not please himself." The sermon's main message was to look out for others instead of for one's own personal interests. A total of 12 individuals, four support staff members, and two ministerial employees were in attendance. The worship service lasted a little over one hour.

I followed my customary approach of starting the message with the Bible in hand. I asked the residents, "What is this in my hand?" They yelled out "The Bible!" One resident interrupted me to share that his mother was in the hospital. I told the resident that I would pray for her, and that the Bible can provide comfort to people when they are sad, sick, or in the hospital. I told the residents, "The Bible is God's special book that tells us how much he loves us."

I read from Romans 15:1-3a. I informed the residents that the Bible verse told everyone that it is important to look out for other people, instead of always looking out for yourself. One resident yelled out that his sister was coming to the Christmas pageant. I affirmed and told the resident, "That is a good example! You can look out for and help your sister through being nice when she comes. You can welcome her and show her around."

I told the residents that they are giving to other people when they sing at chapel service. I added that giving to other people is important, but that it also helps others when you give others an opportunity to play, talk, or sing. One resident informed me that he wanted to play the guitar. I affirmed the resident's previous guitar playing and explained to the resident that he also helped other people out when he let them have a turn as well.

Finally, I thanked the residents for coming and told them that we would see them at the Christmas pageant. The music therapist sang a final song, followed by the closing song, "God Be with You." The residents started to leave, except for one who wanted to stay.

Before the service, Respondent Three and I talked about Christmas gifts and waiting in long lines for rare items before a store opens. This discussion reminded me of the residents. Every Sunday, they wait outside the chapel because they are that excited about coming to church. Before this particular service, I called the residents' homes to tell them to try and encourage the residents to stay until the time of the chapel service due to the inclement weather. While attendance was lower, some residents always attend despite any barriers.

Only Respondents One and Three were available at this chapel service; Respondent Two did not attend. Respondent One commented positively and Respondent Three commented negatively about the residents' body language, verbal cues, and facial expressions. Respondent One observed that several residents talked about the upcoming Christmas party. Four residents were dressed very nicely for church. Respondent One helped two residents with their neckties and one resident with his jacket. A fourth resident showed Respondent One her nice dress, makeup, and shoes. Respondent One observed that the residents enjoyed singing and that the residents in attendance walked to the chapel through drizzling rain and cold weather. Respondent

Three noticed that the repeated behavior of a specific resident visibly frustrated another resident.

Both respondents *agreed* about the participation of the residents in the service. One resident requested a prayer from Respondent One for a sick resident and a staff member who had passed away. Another resident noticed that Respondent Two was not at the chapel service and subsequently asked if she could help by passing bulletins out. Respondent Three observed that almost everyone sang a song with the microphone, two residents danced to a song, and one resident sang passionately despite not knowing a song's words. Respondent One *strongly agreed* and Respondent Three *agreed* that the residents' behaviors showed spiritual engagement. Both respondents commented on residents who danced, sang, and expressed excitement. Respondent One *strongly disagreed* and Respondent Three *disagreed* that the staff demonstrated involvement. Respondent One felt like this was one of the worse services in terms of staff engagement. Respondent One also commented that a staff member who was assigned to a resident with challenging behaviors did not help or redirect the resident at all. Both respondents noticed staff members who were on their phones and sitting in the back of the room.

Both respondents provided *positive* responses concerning the residents' attitudes before and after the service. Respondent One reported that residents smiled and were happy before and after the service. One resident kept expressing concern that he would be late to the Christmas party, which led him to leave early. Another resident did not want to leave once the service finished. Respondent Three felt like the residents seemed relax and noted that one resident enjoyed playing an instrument during the service.

Respondent Three offered *positive* comments regarding how he felt before and after the service. He recorded feelings of contentment before the service; he was happy about changing the music for the service. After the service, he felt focused and ready for the Christmas pageant, which was happening later that afternoon. Respondent One felt *positive* before the service but thought that the weather would impact the attendance. After the service, Respondent One was stressed and frustrated due to a staff member not engaging a resident who experienced behavioral challenges.

Third New Worship Service

The third new worship service took place on Monday, December 5, 2016. The Scripture was Romans 15:1-3a, "We who are strong ought to bear with the failings of the weak and not to please ourselves. Each of us should please his neighbor for his good, to build him up. For even Christ did not please himself." The sermon's main message was that Jesus serves as an example of how to treat others. A total of 17 individuals, four support staff members, three ministerial employees, and two volunteers were in attendance. The worship service lasted 45 minutes.

After the music and prayer portions were finished in the worship service, I announced, "Today we are going to read from the Bible." I informed the congregants that we were going to read from Romans 15:1-3a. Then I asked one of the residents, "We read from Romans last week. Do you remember?" She smiled and said yes, so I went on to read the verse.

I told the residents that the verse talks about helping other people out. I explained that the verse stated that people should not always try to seek selfish gain; people need to think about other people. I told the residents that everyone can do this by saying thank you or singing a song to someone. Chances to help friends out exist throughout the day.

Then I highlighted that the verse cites Jesus as an example of how to be nice. I reminded a resident that the group had earlier sung "Jesus Loves Me." I informed congregants that "Jesus is nice to us because he loves us" and reminded them that the song says "The Bible tells me so." The Bible tells people how Jesus treated others and how they can treat others. One resident said, "Be nice!" I affirmed her and said that everyone needed to be nice. I noted that this is exactly what the verse is telling us: we can be nice to other people.

Lastly, I informed the group that they can be nice and help people every day, just like Jesus did. Then I told them that the music therapist was going to sing a song about loving people, although I knew that the final song was a Christmas song. I did this to play with the music therapist and staff. The music therapist laughed and proceeded to sing.

The residents' excitement at the service and the fact that additional residents attended made me feel like the chaplaincy team was doing something good. The service still seemed a little new to both the residents and the chaplaincy team, so a clear rhythm and expectations were missing. I attributed the newness and lack of expectations as partial causes that the service went longer than planned.

All three respondents provided *positive* statements regarding the participants' body language, verbal cues, and facial expressions. Respondent One recorded that one resident informed him that she had cried earlier in the day. As the music played at the beginning of the service, Respondent One provided pastoral care to the resident. While the emotions expressed by the resident were not positive, her willingness and eagerness to solicit Respondent One's help with her feelings were very good; the resident's desire to confide in Respondent One shows trust and the development of a pastoral relationship. Respondent Two reported that the residents warmly welcomed the chaplaincy team. A few residents also danced, clapped, and sang throughout the service. Respondent Three reported that the residents were on a work break from their normal workshop duties when the chaplaincy team arrived, and their mood seemed lighthearted and relaxed. Respondent Three noticed a few residents smiling and laughing.

Respondents One and Two *strongly agreed* that the residents participated in the service. Respondent One recorded that when one resident saw him, she said, "Church?" as she took his hand and entered the area for the chapel service. Respondent Two reported that the residents willingly engaged in song and prayer time. He noted a specific resident who included fellow residents and the staff when she sang "Whole World." Respondent Three *agreed* that the residents willingly participated in the service. He noted that two residents sat in the back and did not participate, but their eyes were open and they watched. Respondent Three wrote that several residents clapped, laughed, and sung.

Respondents One and Two *strongly agreed* that the residents demonstrated behaviors consistent with spiritual engagement. Respondent One recorded a situation in which a female resident sat in a male resident's seat while he was standing in front to sing. The male resident yelled "You're in my seat!" The female resident apologized and got up. The male resident still looked frustrated. Respondent Three asked him, "Are you going to forgive her?" The male resident calmed down and said, "I forgive you," and the situation ended. Respondent Two noted that many of the residents prayed for family members and talked about loved ones in heaven. Respondent Two assessed that the residents wanted to be in community and continually engaged the ministers and each other. Respondent Three a*greed* that the residents demonstrated spiritual engagement. Respondent Three recorded an interaction in which a resident asked for prayers for her grandmother, which he interpreted as a potential sign of the resident's willingness to confide in him.

Respondents One and Two a*greed* that the staff were involved in the chapel service. Respondent One recorded that two staff members took a break as soon as the service started. This could be a good sign and a way for staff members to benefit from breaks and pastoral care. Once their breaks were over, the staff members returned to the service. One staff member helped calm a resident who was experiencing anxiety. Respondent Two noted that the staff were happy to see the chaplaincy team and both helped and encouraged the residents. Respondent Three d*isagreed* that the staff were involved in the chapel service. He felt like the staff were less engaged in this service than during the two previous services. While he noted that the staff were watchful and observant, he did not see any signs of actual engagement, such as singing, encouraging residents to sing, or clapping.

All three respondents provided *positive* responses concerning the participants' attitudes before and after the service. Respondent One noted that many of the residents shared about their day at first and that several did not want the service to end. Respondent Two reported that the residents were pleasant before the service and that they specifically liked the singing portion. Respondent Three wrote that the residents' attitude was lighthearted and relaxed before the service and upbeat after it.

All three respondents gave *positive* replies concerning how they felt before the service. Respondent Two was happy to engage with the residents on a spiritual and emotional level. Respondent Three wrote that he was angry before the service, due to personal issues. All three respondents provided *positive* replies concerning their post-service feelings. Respondent Two wrote that he was looking forward to the next service. Respondent Three noted that he felt a little less angry after the service because it had provided him a small opportunity to vent.

Fourth Existing Worship Service

The fourth existing chapel service was held on Sunday, December 11, 2016. The Scripture was James 5:16, "Therefore confess your sins to each other and pray for each other so that you may be healed. The prayer of a righteous person is powerful and effective." The sermon's main message was that prayer and confession are part of a community. A total of 27 individuals, five support staff members, and three ministerial employees were in attendance. The service lasted a little over one hour.

Sermon Field Notes for the Fourth Existing Service

I went to the pulpit and asked about the book in my hand. The residents yelled out "That's the

Bible!" Three residents walked up to join me in the pulpit, and I announced to everyone that they would be helping me out. When all three had arrived, I informed everyone that the Bible was God's special book that told people about God and how much He loves them. One of the non-verbal residents present onstage passionately pointed toward the bulletin. I told everyone that the resident was right; the Scripture verse was also in the bulletin that they all had.

I read the Scripture verse and told the congregants that it teaches two things about community or friendship. The first is that prayer is part of a community. I highlighted that everyone had prayed earlier and shared prayer concerns. One resident interrupted to inform me about his mother in the hospital. I expressed concern and reminded the congregation that earlier prayers were offered for his mother during prayer time. Another resident noted that she was sad because her grandmother had died, but she also shared that she loved another resident. I told everyone that she was also right. People can pray when they are sad or about things that make them happy. One of the residents who was onstage started to cry about his father's death. He expressed feelings of responsibility concerning the death and then hugged me. Another resident onstage went over to hug the crying resident. I took the opportunity to point out that the current situation was a good example of friendship and community. People love and pray for each other during both sad and happy times.

Then I told everyone that the second part of friendship and community in the verse is confession. I explained that confession means saying sorry for making a mistake. I shared that I make mistakes, and I try to tell people sorry afterward. I ended by rehashing that praying and saying sorry after making mistakes are two important ways that people are friends at chapel. Finally, I explained that the music therapist would play the closing song, "God Be with You." The residents started to leave, but a few stayed behind to chat with the chaplaincy team.

One of the residents who stayed behind to talk with me wanted to discuss the death of a loved one. I provided pastoral care to her through reflective listening. At the end, the resident said, "I need you to hug me," so I gave her a sideways hug. She smiled, thanked me, and left.

Reflective Entry about the Fourth Existing Service

Prayer is an important part of spirituality for the residents. They seem to easily grasp the concepts of both praying to God and praying for other people. When we talked about prayer as part of the community, the discussion seemed to spark a few residents' grief.

Completed Questionnaires from the Fourth Existing Service

Two *negative* responses were provided regarding the participants' body language, verbal cues, and facial expressions. Respondent One reported that a resident immediately told him about her tough weekend when she first saw him; after the respondent provided pastoral care, the resident seemed calm and relaxed in her speech and body affect. Respondent Two reported a negative incident between two individuals. Resident A sat by Resident B and started to rub her shoulder. Resident B seemed uncomfortable and looked toward Respondent Two for help. Respondent Two intervened and had Resident B move to sit close to him.

Three *positive* responses were offered regarding the residents' body language, verbal cues, and facial expressions. Respondent One reported that a resident had pointed out the sermon section of the pictorial bulletin and noted with enthusiasm, "That's you!" Respondent One affirmed him. Respondent Two recorded that the residents seemed happy and that many had come early to wait for the service. Respondent Three recorded that the residents expressed eagerness about the Christmas party and the opportunity to visit family members.

Respondents One and Two *strongly agreed* that the residents actively participated in the service, while Respondent Three *agreed*. Respondent One reported that so many residents wanted to sing songs that many had to sing together and share the microphone. He also recorded an instance when a resident sat down to join the music therapist as the music therapist played a special song on the piano. The music therapist did not stop, despite the resident continuing to press keys. Respondent Two recorded that many of the residents actively engaged with the sermon and songs. Respondent Three heard fairly lengthy prayers from the residents who were verbal.

Respondents One and Two *strongly agreed* and Respondent Three *agreed* that the residents' behaviors demonstrated spiritual engagement. Respondent One offered examples of the residents politely sharing the microphone. One resident who was very upset at a staff member started to say that she hated the staff member. The music therapist made up a song with the chorus "We love [staff member's name]." The resident started to sing the song and became very happy. Respondent Two reported that many of the residents did not have any reservations during worship. Respondent Three observed that many residents approached the chaplain during the sermon to engage him.

Respondents One and Three *agreed* and Respondent Two *disagreed* that the staff were involved with the residents. Respondent One reported that many of the staff members were talking with the chaplain and residents freely and inclusively. Respondent Three provided an example of a staff member walking up to a resident who was crying on the stage. The staff member asked the resident to sit by her and then spent the rest of the service talking with her. Respondent Two noticed a staff member on her phone throughout the service and thinks that this individual may view the service as a time for staff relaxation and a break.

All of the respondents gave *positive* answers regarding the participants' attitudes before and after the service. Respondent One reported that many of the residents shared about their holiday plans. He recorded that one resident visited me after the service to seek pastoral care for grief.

Respondent Two noted that many residents were excited before and after the service. One resident did not want to go home, but the ministers assured her that she could return to chapel the following week. This approach seemed to help, and the resident eventually left willingly. Respondent Three observed excitement and noted that most residents left fairly quickly after the service.

Respondent Three recorded that he felt tired and passive before the service but engaged, active, and awake after it. Respondent One felt good before the service; afterward he felt relieved and nervous that it was the last Sunday for formal evaluations. Respondent Two felt happy and connected both before and after the service.

Fourth New Worship Service

The fourth new worship service occurred on Monday, December 12, 2016. The Scripture was James 5:16, "Therefore confess your sins to each other and pray for each other so that you may be healed. The prayer of a righteous person is powerful and effective." The sermon's main message was that offering prayer is a way to prepare for Christmas. A total of 16 individuals, six staff members, three ministerial employees, and two volunteers were in attendance. The service lasted 40 minutes.

Sermon Field Notes for the Fourth New Service

I started by asking what was coming up in two weeks. One resident said, "My momma!" I affirmed her by saying that the resident would see her mother soon. Another person said that he would see his father soon. Finally, a third stated that his mother had died. I expressed condolences. The resident then reported that his mother had died a year ago and that he feels sad. I provided pastoral support and attentive listening.

Then I redirected the participants. I told them that Christmas is coming within two weeks and that Christmas gets us thinking about our loved ones. Someone mentioned the Christmas party. I expressed excitement and told the group that I was also going to the party. Several residents became thrilled as they talked about the party and gifts. I told the residents that people can say thank you when others give gifts, adding that they can also thank God because He provides gifts.

I reminded the congregants of the music therapist's final song, "Emmanuel," and told them that people celebrate Christmas because of Jesus' birthday. I explained that as everyone thinks about Christmas and God being with us, everyone can pray to help—which prepares hearts and expresses thanks. I read James 5:16 and explained that when people pray for another person it is like giving that individual a gift. I affirmed that prayers are an important part of preparing for Christmas and saying thank you to God and others. A resident conveyed gratitude and excitement for what she expected to receive for Christmas. I expressed enthusiasm with her and explained that the resident could pray both for the person giving her the gift and to thank God.

Finally, I told the group that it was the last Monday service. I thanked everyone for their time and invited them to participate in the Sunday chapel service. The staff and residents thanked the chaplaincy team, and the chaplaincy team left.

Reflective Entry about the Fourth New Service

Internally, I found it difficult to say goodbye and felt a mixture of sadness and guilt. I wanted to keep this service going but does not think that the chaplaincy team can add to its current load of 12 to 16 chapel services a week. I will miss this group and the Monday service.

Completed Questionnaires from the Fourth New Service

Respondent One offered *positive* observations about the residents' body language, verbal cues, and expressions. He reported that they yelled out songs, eagerly shared prayer requests, and were engaged with the sermon. Respondent Two mentioned that the residents happily greeted the chaplaincy team using handshakes and verbal welcomes. Respondent Three highlighted that many residents went to the front of the room to sing songs. However, he also made one *neutral* comment: he noticed that one resident moved her finger in a circular motion at her head and pointed to another resident, as if to say he was "crazy."

Respondents One and Two *strongly agreed* and Respondent Three *agreed* that the residents participated in the service. One resident intentionally joked and laughed with the chaplain by acting like he did not know the music therapist or the chaplaincy assistant. Respondent Two noted that one resident followed the chaplaincy assistant throughout prayer time to hold his hand and touch the communication device. Respondent Three noted that one resident initiated a song on his own and that many residents prayed and sang.

Respondents One and Two *strongly agreed* and Respondent Three *agreed* that the residents' behaviors showed spiritual engagement. One resident noticed Respondent One taking field notes and informed him that she wanted him to write something on a piece of paper for her. When Respondent One inquired further, the resident asked that he write her a prayer. The first prayer that the respondent wrote was simple and apparently too short as the resident handed it back and said she wanted a longer prayer; the respondent then added the Lord's Prayer to the paper. Respondent Two noted that the residents demonstrated joy about the Christmas party and that the chaplain had effectively incorporated the residents' input into the message. Respondent Three reported that a resident asked a prayer for the staff member who worked with her and that many residents expressed joy in their own way.

Respondents One and Three a*greed* that the support staff expressed involvement while Respondent Two *strongly agreed*. Respondent One noticed that two staff members took breaks when they arrived and that the chaplain bantered with a resident and staff member. Respondent Two witnessed staff engagement through body affect and noticed the volunteers encouraging the residents. Respondent Three noted that one volunteer told a resident that she had a beautiful voice and that a staff member helped to set chairs out.

Respondent One offered *positive* comments regarding the participants' attitudes before and after the service. He noted that residents smiled when they arrived and that a few residents had held his hand. Respondent Two felt like the residents were excited before and after the service. Respondent Three recorded that the residents' level of excitement was high at both junctures.

Respondent One felt happy before the chapel service. While the chaplaincy team was walking to the chapel service, they ran into a speech therapist—who I invited to join us. She accepted the invitation and sang, clapped, and signed throughout the service. After the service, Respondent One felt happy with a mixture of sadness and guilt (given that the new chapel service was coming to an end). Respondent Two felt excited and happy both before and after the service. Respondent Three felt happy before the service but a little mad after, because a piece of paper that he needed was accidently taken and used for something else. He later discovered that Respondent One had used it to write prayers for a resident (as described above).

Evaluating my Project
The central question for this spiritual formation guide was how people with intellectual disabilities grow spiritually. My main thesis is

that relationships are the primary way in which people with cognitive impairments develop spiritually. An evaluation of existing and new chapel services provides the primary application of the spiritual formation guide's teachings. This evaluation section discusses the results, which includes highlighting the difference and similarities between the new and existing chapel services, and my concluding thoughts.

Results from the Chapel Services

The project involved three respondents and eight chapel services, which led to a total of twenty-four completed questionnaires. The four tables presented below summarize the questionnaire responses that the respondents provided following each service. Each response is given the value of one point. In cases in which a respondent selected two answers, I assigned each response a value of 0.5 instead of a full point. Table 1 provides the Likert-scale results for the questionnaires completed after each existing chapel service.

Table 1. Likert-scale responses on the questionnaires for the existing chapel service

	Strongly Agree	Agree	N/A	Disagree	Strongly Disagree
Q.2	10	1	1	0	0
Q.3	7	4	1	0	0
Q.4	1	6.5	1	2.5	1

Three questions use a Likert-scale. Question two regards the residents' level of participation and question three assesses if they were engaged spiritually; in both cases, a positive answer of *strongly agree* or *agree* signifies spiritual growth. Table 1 illustrates that the only area of disagreement among the respondents in relation to any of these factors concerns the level of the support staff's involvement, for a total of 3.5 answers. The three *N/A* responses reflect the fact that Respondent Two missed one service. The majority of responses for the questions are *strongly agree* (18) and *agree* (11.5).

While Table 1 focuses on the existing service, Table 2 illustrates the Likert-scale results for the questionnaires completed after each new chapel service.

Table 2. Likert-scale responses on the questionnaires for the new chapel service

	Strongly Agree	Agree	N/A	Disagree	Strongly Disagree
Q.2	7	5	0	0	0
Q.3	8	4	0	0	0
Q.4	2	9	0	1	0

Once again, the only area of *disagree* comes from question four, which deals with staff involvement. A total of 17 *strongly agree* with 18 *agree* responses were provided, which means that the services elicited very similar reactions from the residents; Table 2 just has slightly more *agree* and *strongly agree* responses (with 35 *positive* responses in comparison to the 29.5 in Table 1). Moreover, the existing chapel service in Table 1 has more *negative* responses with 3.5

compared to the one *negative* response for the new chapel service in Table 2.

In addition to the Likert-scale questions, I also used open-ended questions to evaluate the two services. Question one deals with the residents' body language, verbal cues, and the facial expressions; question five concerns participants' attitudes before and after the service; and question six, which is reflective in nature, allows the respondent to assess his or her personal attitude before and after the chapel service. Table 3 provides the four-week totals of the responses to the open-ended questions for the existing chapel service.

Table 3. Responses to open-ended questions concerning the existing chapel service

	Positive	Neutral	Negative	N/A
Q.1	8.5	1	1.5	1
Q.5	10.5	0	.5	1
Q.6	7	0	4	1

The respondents' answers were categorized as *positive, neutral,* or *negative.* The residents sometimes offered answers that contained mixed *positive, neutral,* or *negative* responses; as a result, I divided the responses into decimal points. The *N/A* response is due to Respondent Two's absence from one existing service. The existing chapel services had a total of 26 *positive,* one *neutral,* and six *negative* responses.

Most of the *negative* responses (namely four) center on question six, which deals with how the respondent felt before and after the service. With the exception of one incident, all of the *negative* responses related to how the respondents felt before a service. Reviewing the completed evaluations revealed that when the respondents reported feeling *negative* before a service, 66% of the time they recorded having *positive* feelings after it.

From Table 3, it appears that the residents mostly exhibited *positive* body language (8.5 times); in contrast, they *negative* and *neutral* body language 1.5 times and once, respectively. From the respondents' replies, the residents seem generally happy to attend and participate in the existing chapel service and demonstrate this attitude both verbally and non-verbally.

Table 4 outlines the questionnaire responses to the same open-ended questions but in relation to the new chapel service.

Table 4. Responses to open-ended questions concerning the new chapel service

	Positive	Neutral	Negative	N/A
Q.1	9.5	.5	2	0
Q.5	11.5	0	.5	0
Q.6	9.5	0	2.5	0

As with the Likert-scale questions, the new chapel service scored slightly better than the existing chapel service on the questionnaire. The existing chapel service had 26 *positive*, one *neutral*, and six *negative* responses, while the new chapel service had 30.5 *positive*, 0.5 *neutral*, and five *negative* responses. The completed evaluations also revealed that when the respondents recorded having *negative* feelings before a new chapel service, 75% of the time their feelings changed to *positive* feelings after the service.

It appears that a common factor between the existing and new chapel services is that the respondents change from *negative* to *positive* feelings before and after a service (66% of the time with the existing service and 75% of the time with the new service). The chapel services therefore help the respondents feel better. A gift that people with intellectual disabilities can offer the larger religious community may be positively impacting the mood of others through worshipping with them.

Based on the evaluation of the new and existing chapel services, the teachings from the spiritual formation guide help people with intellectual disabilities to grow—even to the point that the new chapel service produced greater results than the existing chapel service. I found this very surprising, specifically considering that the existing chapel service has been around longer and has more to offer: it is preceded by a 45-minute fellowship time, features microphones and more complex music, and is held in the chapel.

I also noticed an interesting connection between intellect and relationships. Reflecting on my field notes and observations of others from the chaplaincy team helped me to notice that the residents often understood and were able to provide answers that were consistent with the sermon message; many of them yelled correct answers out or applied the message to their own lives during the sermon. The residents' involvement was made possible because the relationship between the ministers and residents had been developed beforehand. As suggested in the theological rationale, the residents were able to incorporate basic parts of the Bible into their daily living.

Concluding Thoughts

The project gave rise to a few opportunities to bring about changes in my practices and thinking. The first area concerns measuring the effectiveness of service. One of the criteria of the evaluation of the spiritual formation guide was the support staff's involvement. I am convinced that staff involvement helps the residents to worship and grow spiritually. Staff assisting residents at worship services communicates God's care. People with intellectual disabilities are the same as people without disabilities, but the former need additional support. As this statement is also true in the spiritual life, the involvement of a support staff member helps to facilitate residents' spiritual growth and engagement.

While support staff involvement is indeed crucial, be cautious because it can be overemphasized. It may not be fair to judge the support staff's participation or even have it as a main factor for ministry success. Staff members may not want to participate in the worship services for many reasons, including that they do not know how to help. Most staff are conditioned that church is a place where people sit and listen. If you are going to expect staff to participate more, you must establish some formalized training for them. This spiritual formation guide can serve that purpose.

A second reason that support staff may not want to participate is because they are spiritually wounded or have deeply held convictions. While you may be comfortable from various faith backgrounds, a staff person without exposure or experience may not be. As I reflected on staff involvement, I remembered a previous instance in which a staff member stated that she could not come into the chapel; I observed that she was visibly upset and on the verge of tears. I honored her request and provided pastoral care to her. While this example may be extreme, other support staff could have spiritual wounding from religious leaders or organizations. Our role is to also offer pastoral care to staff members needs. If we are relying on their involvement as a matrix for our success, then we are not setting the support staff up for spiritual healing.

We can intentionally apply the spiritual formation guide's relational concepts to the staff for spiritual health and healing. Relationships are a foundational part of spiritual development, whether someone has or does not have a disability. We can look for opportunities to use the approaches in the guide (e.g., relational discipleship, laughter, and empathy) to connect with and come alongside the support staff.

The new chapel service yielded slightly better results than the existing chapel service, which leads me to believe that 30 minutes may perhaps be a good length for a chapel service. Although the chaplaincy team tried to use the longer services to accommodate everyone, the project's results seem to indicate that a compressed time produces better results.

The project's findings are that a relational spiritual formation model is effective for adults with intellectual disabilities. Even in a new setting, employing this spiritual formation guide can yield almost immediate results. The findings are important for the future because others who minister with—or are interested in ministering with—persons with intellectual disabilities have been provided a new ministry tool.

People with intellectual disabilities have much to both contribute to and receive from the church. This relationship-based spiritual formation plan develops a reciprocal connection in which the religious community can grow both together and with God. This guide illustrates that the effects of a relational approach positively impact the spiritual life and involvement of people who have intellectual disabilities. Hopefully, the church will engage and partner with people who have intellectual disabilities for the development of the Body of Christ.

Main Areas for Evaluation of Ministry

1. Does the ministry help people feel connected with the Divine?

2. Does the ministry connect people with each other?

3. Is the ministry honoring and does it bring dignity to people who have intellectual disabilities?

4. Does the ministry help people cope?

5. Does the ministry and worship services allow for personal choice?

6. Does the ministry recognize the gifts, talents, and contributions of everyone?

Evaluation of Spiritual Formation Guide at the
Worship Services

1. Examine the thoughts, feelings, and
observations of the participants such as body
language, verbal cues, and facial
expression. Please list a pseudonym for anyone
that stood out to you.

2. The congregants willingly participated and
engaged in the service.
    Strongly Agree
    Agree
    Not Applicable
    Disagree
    Strongly Disagree

Additional Comments:

3. Do the behaviors of the participants
demonstrate that they are engaged spiritually?
More specifically, are the people showing joyous
expressions, do they demonstrate a willingness
to confide or engage with the minister, and are
the individuals free to express themselves
through worship?
    Strongly Agree
    Agree
    Not Applicable
    Disagree
    Strongly Disagree

Additional Comments:

4. What is the level of involvement or engagement of the support staff? Are the support staff assisting the individuals? Do they seem engaged through body affect?

    Strongly Agree
    Agree
    Not Applicable
    Disagree
    Strongly Disagree

Additional Comments:

5. What is the attitude and expression of the participants before and after the service?

6. How do you feel before and after the service?

WORKS CITED

Aigen, Kenneth. "A Critique of Evidence-Based Practice in Music Therapy." *Music Therapy Perspectives* 33, no.1 (2015): 12-24.

Andurus, David. "Theology and Its Impact on People with Disability: An Ecclesiology Inclusive of People with a Disability." *Missio Apostolica* (2003): 143-149.

Aronowitz, Robert, Andrew Deener, Danya Keene, Jason Schnittker, and Laura Tach. "Cultural Reflexibity in Health Research and Practice." *American Journal of Public Health* 105, no.53 (2015): 403-408.

Baker, John. "Spiritual Education in the Special School Setting for Pupils with Learning Difficulties/Disabilities." *International Journal of Children's Spirituality* 17, no. 2 (May 2012): 153-166.

Basselin, Tim. "Why Theology Needs Disability." *Theology Today* 68 (2011): 47-57.

Benner, David G. *Presence and Encounter: The Sacramental Possibilities of Everyday Life.* Grand Rapids: Brazos Press, 2014.

Binau, Brad A. "Pastoral Theology for the Missional Church: From Pastoral Care to the Care of Souls." *Trinity Seminary Review* 34, no.1 (Spring 2014): 11-28.

Boisen, Anton. *The Exploration of the Inner World: A Study of Mental Disorder and Religious Experience.* Philadelphia: University of Pennsylvania Press, 1971.

Boyce, James L. "A Mirror of Identity: Implanted Word and Pure Religion in James 1:17-27." *Word & World* 35, no.3 (Summer 2015): 213-221.

Carter, Erik W., Harold L. Kleinhert, Tony F. LoBianco, Kathleen Sheppard-Jones, Laura N. Butler, and Milton S. Tyree. "Congregational Participation of a National Sample of Adults with Intellectual and Developmental Disabilities." *Intellectual and Developmental Disabilities* 53 (2015): 381-393.

Christiani, Tabita Kartika. "Doing Theology: Towards the Construction of Methods for Living with Disability." *Asia Journal of Theology* 28, no. 1 (April 2014): 35-58.

Cohoon, Wesley D. "A Relationship-Based Spiritual Formation Plan for Adults with Intellectual Disabilities." Doctor of Ministry Project. Abilene: Logsdon Seminary, 2017.

Danforth, Scot. "Liberation Theology of Disability and the Option for the Poor." *Disability Studies Quarterly* 25, no. 3 (Summer 2005).

Ersahin, Zehra. "The Elephant in the Room: Implications of the on-going Conflict Between Religion and Science, and What Pluralism Offers Working with the (in) visible." *Counseling Psychology Review* 28, no.2 (June 2013): 39-50.

Fee, Gordon D. *The First Epistle of the Corinthians: Revised Edition.* The New International Commentary of the New Testament .Grand Rapids: William B. Eerdmans Publishing Company, 2014.

Goh, Anita, Tamara Eagleton, Rosemary Kelleher, Olga Yasturbetskaya, Michael Taylor, Edmond Chiu, Bridget Hamilton, Tom Trauer, and Nicola T. Lautenschlager. "Pastoral Care in Old Age Psychiatry: Addressing the Spiritual Needs of Inpatients in an Acute Aged Mental Health Unit." *Asia-Pacific Psychiatry* 6, (2015): 127-134.

Graves, Thomas H. "The Role of Despair and Anger in Christian Spirituality." *Review & Expositor* 113, no.2 (May 2016): 181-197.

Haslam, Molly C. *A Constructive Theology of Intellectual Disability: Human Being as Mutuality and Response.* New York: Fordham University Press, 2012.

Hobbs, Richard, Jennifer Fogo, and C. Elizabeth Bonham. "Individuals with Disabilities: Critical Factors that Facilitate Integration in Christian Religious Communities." *Journal of Rehabilitation* 82, no.1 (2016): 36-46.

Hooper, Jeff, Tony Wigram, Derek Carson, and Bill Lindsay. "The Practical Implications of Comparing How Adults with and Without Intellectual Disability Respond to Music." *British Journal of Learning Disabilities* 39 (2010): 22-28.

Johnson, Hilary, Jacinta Douglas, Christine Bigby, and Teresa Iacono. "A Model of Processes that Underpin Positive Relationships for Adults with Severe Intellectual Disability." *Journal of Intellectual & Developmental Disability* 37, no.4 (December 2012): 324-336.

Lee, Juyoung. "A Phenomenological Study of the Interpersonal Relationships Between Five Music Therapists and Adults with Profound Intellectual and Multiple Disabilities." *Qualitative Inquiries in Music Therapy* 9 (2014): 43-86.

Lifshitz-Vahav, Hefziba. "Compensation Age Theory: Effect of Chronological Age on Individuals with Intellectual Disability." *Education and Training in Autism and Disabilities* 50, no.2 (June 2015): 142-154.

Manual Writing Committee. "Standards 311-312
    Outcomes of CPE Level I/Level II Programs.
    Pastoral Competence: 312.6." *ACPE
    Standards & Manuals.* Decatur: Association
    of Clinical Pastoral Education, Inc., 2016.
    Accessed on July 18, 2016,
    www.acpe.edu/ACPE/Resources/Resources
    _.aspx.

McKnight, Scot. *The Letter of James.* The New
    International Commentary of the New
    Testament. Grand Rapids: William B.
    Eerdmans Publishing Company, 2011.

McNair, Jeff. "Disability Studies Applied to
    Disability Ministry." *Review & Expositor*
    113, no. 2 (May 2016): 159-166.

Morris, Leon. *The Gospel According to Matthew.*
    Grand Rapids: William B. Eerdmans
    Publishing Company, 1992.

Murray, Stuart. *The Naked Anabaptist: The Bare
    Essentials of a Radical Faith.* Scottdale:
    Herald Press, 2010.

Nogalski, James D. *The Book of the Twelve:
    Micah-Malachi.* Smyth & Helwys Bible
    Commentary. Macon: Smyth & Helwys
    Publishing Inc., 2011.

Palmer, Parker J. *Let Your Life Speak: Listening
    for the Voice of Vocation.* San Francisco:
    Jossey-Bass Publishers, 1999.

Pembroke, Neil. "Witness to Hope in the Christian Community Through Irony." *Pastoral Psychology* 58 (2009): 433-443.

Regan, Ethna. *Theology and the Boundary Discourse of Human Rights.* Washington: Georgetown University Press, 2010.

Reinders, Hans S. *Disability, Providence, and Ethics: Bridging Gaps, Transforming Lives.* Waco: Baylor University Press, 2014.

Reynolds, Thomas E. *Vulnerable Communion: A Theology of Disability and Hospitality.* Grand Rapids: Brazos Press, 2008.

Riddoch, Jane V. and Russell F. Waugh. "Teaching Students with Severe Intellectual Disabilities Non-Representational Art Using a New Pictorial and Music Programme." *Journal of Intellectual & Developmental Disability* 28, no.2 (June 2003): 145-162.

Root, Andrew. *The Relational Pastor: Sharing in Christ by Sharing Ourselves.* Downers Grove: InterVarsity Press, 2013.

Schurter, Dennis D. *A Mutual Ministry: Theological Reflections and Resources on Ministry with People with Mental Retardation and Other Disabilities.* Denton: Dennis D. Schurter, 1994.

Slocum, Victoria. "Recommendations for Including People with Intellectual Disabilities in Faith Communities." *Christian Education Journal* 13, no.1 (2016): 109-126.

Snow-Flesher, LeAnn. "Mercy Triumphs Over Judgment: James as Social Gospel." *Review & Expositor* 111, no.2 (May 2014): 180-186.

Streets, Fredrick, J. "Love: A Philosophy for Pastoral Care and Counseling." *Verbum et Ecclesia* 2, no.35 (2014), 1-11.

Swinton, John. "Who is the God We Worship? Theologies of Disability; Challenges and New Possibilities." *International Journal of Practical Theology* 14 (February 2011): 273-307.

Waltke, Bruce K. *A Commentary on Micah.* Grand Rapids: William B. Eerdmans Publishing Company, 2007.

Wehmeyer, Michael L. *The Story of Intellectual Disability: An Evolution of Meaning, Understanding, & Public Perception.* Baltimore: Paul H. Brooks Publishing Co., 2013.

Whitt, Jason D. "In the Image of God: Receiving Children with Special Needs." *Review & Expositor* 113, no. 2 (May 2016): 205-216.

Yong, Amos. *The Bible, Disability, and the Church: A New Vision of the People of God.* Grand Rapids: William B. Eerdmans Publishing Company, 2011.

Made in the USA
Monee, IL
07 January 2023

24735593R00066